MW01279836

PUBLISHED *by* PARABLES

Earthly Stories with a Heavenly Meaning

EAGLE CHRISTIANITY

BY

ANTHONY RITTHALER

PUBLISHED by PARABLES
Earthly Stories with a Heavenly Meaning

Eagle Christianity
Author - Anthony Ritthaler

Copyright Anthony Ritthaler
October, 2018

Published By Parables
October, 2018

ISBN 978-1-945698-80-4
Printed in the United States of America

Eagle Christianity

By

Anthony Ritthaler

PUBLISHED *by* PARABLES
Earthly Stories with a Heavenly Meaning

TABLE OF CONTENTS

INTERESTING FACTS
ABOUT EAGLES

- There are 60 different types of eagles around the world.
- In the 1700s there were around 300 thousand to 500 thousand bald eagles in America. By late 1978 they were on the endangered species list. Now there are around 70,000 bald eagles in North America.
- It's possible for eagles to live up to 70 years.
- Eagles have holes in their tongues.
- Eagles do not sweat.
- Eagle's body temperature is 106 degrees Fahrenheit and they can be found in all continents except Antarctica.
- Eagles have eyesight that is much stronger than humans and they can see 5 colors.
- Eagles have hollow bones and they are very light.
- Ninety percent of eagles have one mate for life but if one dies they will quickly find another mate.
- It's against federal law to own even an eagle feather if caught you could pay up to 5,000 dollars.
- The bald eagle has been the national bird of America since 1782.
- Eagles have no teeth.
- Female eagles always weigh more than males. Females weigh on average 12 pounds. Males, on average, weigh 9 pounds.

- Bald eagles have around 7,000 feathers.
- Female bald eagles can have a wingspan of up to 8 feet.
- Eagles can travel up to 125 miles a day if need be and it glides majority of the time.
- All eagles are fully mature at 5 years old and look the same as older bald eagles.
- Eagles only eat meat.
- Eagles are not only great in the air but they are excellent swimmers too and Eagles can sleep standing up.
- They can fly up to 10,000 feet.
- Eagles are at the top of their food chain and are some of the most powerful birds on Earth.
- The average bald eagle nest is 4-5 feet deep and each year an adult will add 1-2 feet of new material to the nest. The largest nest ever recorded was in Florida. It was 9.5 feet in diameter and 20 feet deep and weighed nearly 3 tons.
- Eagles hold the record for the largest load known to be carried by a flying bird. It was a bald eagle which flew with a 15 pound mule deer fawn.
- The largest known kill by an eagle was a dunker deer, weighing 82 pounds.
- Eagles dive at incredible speeds and have supernatural grip pressure.
- Eagles grow very fast and at 6 weeks weigh about 8 to 9 pounds.

- Eagles have small but strong stomachs and they have something called a crop that can hold up to 2 pounds of fish.
- Eagles have three eyelids.
- They can see other eagles from 50 miles away.
- They can dive at speeds of 125 to 200 miles per hour.
- They love storms.
- Lastly they love to do tricks in the air and they enjoy life.

Enjoy the book everyone!

Special Thanks

When I think about this book and all my books in general I'm thankful to God above for His help and guidance in writing them.

From my first book to the book you are about to read I've tried to make sure Jesus, above anything else, is lifted up and honored as much as possible. God has provided three important things that has been vital to the success of this feeble ministry and I would like to mention them now.

The first thing God has provided is his imprint on this ministry.

Without His touch all ministries will fail and from the start I've sought his approval on this ministry and I'm humbled that He has done things only He could do. God has sent clear cut stamps of approval that have left others speechless and He deserves all the glory. He has opened up radio, done miracles, and touched hearts all over the world. God's hand has moved on so many hearts and the more He is raised up the more impact ministries will have too touch hearts. We should all seek His approval not mans and if we make that our main goal things will always happen.

The second thing I want to thank God for is inspiration. The Bible says holy men of God spoke as they were moved by the Holy Ghost. When I write I want to get out of the way and allow Gods hand to move my hand. Authors all around the country cannot believe or understand how I wrote books in such short time and all I can say is with God all things are possible. Without inspiration from above writing is very difficult but with

His help it can flow like a river. God is the one that gives ability without his assistance it is not possible. My desire is to honor God, and trust that God will give the words to say and because I think that way God gives the grace needed to make it happen. I've never went to school for writing but who needs school when you can get personal lessons from the author of peace Himself. Thanks be unto Jesus for His touch that gives the words of eternal comfort to the broken heart.

The last thing I would like to mention that God has provided is insight. As I write I rely on God's wisdom and insight to take over because that's the only hope this world has to get help, not my wisdom, but Gods. People tell me often that when they read these books the Holy Ghost grabs their heart and refreshes their minds. With all books I pen I try to flood them with God's words not mine. Folks we need wisdom from Heaven and without God's word that will never happen.

These three things I mentioned is absolutely a must to see hearts altered for the glory of God. The old song writer said "All is vain unless the spirit of the Holy one comes down." There is nothing more true than that statement and until we discover this truth we will never reach others for Christ.

Thank you Lord for all you have done.

INTRODUCTION

In God's word there is a gold standard or principle for Christian living and it is found in the eagle. Eagles possess rare physical gifts that shine like a lighthouse and we as Christians need to exam these gifts and apply them to our spiritual lives. The only life God desires for His children is the spirit filled life and as we study the greatness of the eagle I hope we learn how to soar like we never have before. There are many verses in God's word that point us to freedom, power and liberty and to not have a desire to achieve this status is very foolish on our part. Eagle Christianity is rare to achieve but through this book I pray God gives us all a longing to reach for higher ground with God.

We will look at eagle's habits, attributes, gifts, and methods that propel them to greatness and cause them to excel over their enemies. Eagles are born to fly high and as Christians we are meant to do the same thing.

We will examine the eagle and see from Gods word how they live in such victory. As God's children we need to add the eagle's physical qualities to our own walk with God. If we have a strong desire to fly with God we must continue to grow with God and use the eagle as our example.

Eagles have always stood for freedom, anointing, power and beauty and the only way we can reach this level is through old fashion hard work and submission to God. Eagles are extremely rare and if you reach this level you may find yourself alone but to be alone with Jesus is far better than being in the company of others who will never fly.

May this book inspire you to reach for the stars spiritually and I pray that many more bald eagles will rise out of the shadows of the cold Christian life and soar towards the revival fires of the Son. Allow the Lord to reveal to you how special you can be for Him through the truths of this book. It's about time that we stop hanging with turkeys and start soaring with eagles.

Enjoy this book and learn how to live a life of victory, confidence and boldness through the help of the Lord. Eagle Christianity is missing and until we pay the price for God true revival will be a thing of the past.

CHAPTER 1:

To Have Eagle Christianity We Must Hunger After Vision From Above

Probably the most breathtaking physical quality of the eagle is the incredible vision God has given them. Everything about its vision is breath taking and it grants them an amazing advantage in life.

Humans with perfect vision have 20/20 vision, while an eagle has 20/4 vision meaning that what we can see clearly at twenty feet away an eagle can see at hundred feet away. Experts say that an eagle can spot a mouse or rabbit from a little over two miles away. Our eyes as human take up about five percent of our head, but an eagles eyes occupy about fifty percent of their head.

An eagle's vision is four to five times better than humans with a much wider vision as well. As humans we see three basic colors, while an eagle can see five including the ability to see ultraviolet light. Humans have around 200,000 light sensitive cells per millimeter of their retina, while an eagle has about 1 million light sensitive cells per square millimeter of their retina. An eagle can see fish under the water and scoop down and grab them.

Experts say that eagle's eyes are so strong they could see an ant from the top of a ten story building. God has given these wonderful creatures eye sight physically that, we as Christians, should all seek spiritually.

As God's children we all should study an eagle's vision and try our best to spiritually see past our noses in the work of God. All across America and even the world,

Christians are near sighted and seemly only concerned with their own surroundings and own church. Jesus has commanded us to launch out into the deep, and also to be fishers of men, according to Matthew 4:19.

The precious Word of God says in Proverbs 29:18, "Where there is no vision the people perish." All over this planet people dwell in chains of depravity and we are commanded to reach the world with the gospel of Jesus Christ. The Scriptures instructs us to go ye into all the world, and preach the gospel to every creature. That my friends is a great vision and if we want to develop eyesight spiritually, like the eagle has physically, we must have a hunger to reach the world.

Having vision like the Bible teaches is not just reaching others around you while you live, but it is having a ministry that reaches hearts long after you leave Earth. When I think of vision for God I think of people like Fanny Crosby, who wrote 9,000 songs and they are still reaching hearts many years after her death. Mrs. Crosby always thought about other people and other ministries and died with just sixty-three dollars while living next to a rescue mission because that's where her heart lived spiritually.

When I think of vision for the Lord I also think of Ford Porter, who for nine long years prayed God would give him a ministry that would reach souls long after his death. God gave him the words to write a gospel track called "God's Simple Plan of Salvation," that has been printed 680 billion times now and has covered the world.

Christians in these last days have lost their vision for God and people are dropping off into Hell in record numbers. The biggest danger of pastors, missionaries, evangelists, and saints today is getting wrapped up only in their ministries while people all around the world go without. Jesus wants us to see the world how He sees it, not how we want to see it.

An eagle will have victories, triumphs and overwhelming success consistently, all throughout their lives due to vision from another world. Every morning we get out of bed we should fall on our knees and beg God to give us great vision for the world around us and if we do a new world will begin to open up for us.

It will be a great day in our Christian life when we realize that if our vision increases, fruit for God will too. May we all see how the eagle looks at life and take a page form their book. We may not understand it now but when we arrive in glory we will see it rather quickly.

People who soared for God through vision and others who made it there but had nothing to cast at Jesus' feet. Many will stand in ashes of regret because on Earth they had no vision for the lost, while others will be honored because their vision was right. Allow your vision to grow year in and year out and you will start to experience eagle Christianity.

CHAPTER 2:

To Be an Eagle Christian We Must Be Strong in the Lord

When you study the life of an eagle you quickly discover that they are very strong. Scientists and experts say that an eagle has around 10 times more grip pressure than humans do. The eagle relies on its God given strength to overwhelm its enemies and once it gets a hold of them there is really no escaping their strong grip. Eagles are extremely powerful and their strength separates them in many ways from other birds.

As Christians, God in heaven desires to turn us into strong warriors for Him. Many saints of God make the awful mistake of trying to fight life's battles in the energy of the flesh rather than in the strength of the Lord. This mindset results in defeated lives and failure to the max degree.

God wants us to walk in His strength daily and He is willing and able to give us great strength from above. The Bible says in Ephesians 6:10, "Finally my brethren, be strong in the Lord, and in the power of His might." Without God's touch upon our lives we will always be weak, frail, and lacking in our walk with Him.

The Bible says in Isaiah 26:4, "Trust ye in the Lord forever: for in the Lord Jehovah is everlasting strength." The wonderful thing about having God's strength is the fact that it's never ending and it's everlasting. We all must learn that within ourselves we can do nothing but with God's help there is nothing we cannot do.

The Bible says this in Philippians 4:13, "I can do all things through Christ, which strengtheneth me." Eagles are strong, eagles are confident, and because of it they are the king of the air. Most Christians we meet in these last days are not strong, they have no confidence in God and therefore the devil kicks them around like a soccer ball.

God has given us all the tools from His word to make us strong but it's up to us to grow stronger for Him no one can do it for us. The only way to defeat the devil is to be strong in the Lord and to hide under the shadow of His wings. Allow God to fight your battles through the strength that He offers.

Eagles are victors, they are winners, and it's largely because their strength increases from year to year. How often do we grow stronger in the Lord? That is a question we should ask ourselves every day. God wants us to be strong like an eagle and He wants us to seek His power daily.

If we could add the strength of the Lord to our lives, flying with God would be just around the corner. Thank God for the examples eagles set and would to God we all go after the strength of Almighty God.

CHAPTER 3:

To Have Eagle Christianity You Must Have Laser-Like Focus

It is impossible to achieve levels of greatness without laser-like focus. A huge part of the eagle's success is its ability to lock in on prey and never let it out of its sight. Once an eagle determines to focus in on something nothing distracts them from accomplishing their goal. Eagles are winners because they are always focused and they triumph over others who lack the same focus.

All across the world, today Christians struggle because the devil has took away people's focus. We are living in days of divine distractions and people's minds are on everything but God. When I walk through the doors of the church people come to me telling me about sports, their weekend, the weather, their problems, their money situation, what they watched on tv, their family, their week and when that's all over they may talk about church and God.

Years ago when revival swept across this country people had supreme focus on one thing in church and that was God. I've read about many revivals where a preacher could stand up and preach for 3 straight hours and people never lost focus and never wanted the service to end. People were hungry for God and they were not in a hurry when they got to church. If revival extended week after week people would weep with excitement and they would gladly attend every night.

Years ago, people centered their life and focus towards God and they had eagle-like focus and lives by the untold thousands were transformed. Statistics say about 17% of what a preacher says is comprehended by the people. Statistics also reveal the attention span of the average member of a church is about 20 minutes.

When people sit in church their minds are controlled by other things except God and lack of focus has destroyed this world. Many preachers are dropping dead because they can't get people to care about the church and the things of God. When you invite folks out to church they come up with every excuse in the world because the devil has their mind not God.

Folks must be entertained in these last days and if they are not entertained in church they refuse to come. Statistics say that the average house hold owns 24 electronic devices and they are feeding their minds with trash that fights against God. A teen once told me, he sleeps for 8 hours a day and watches tv, plays on the internet, and uses his phone for a total of 12 hours a day.

The devil has stolen people's focus and instead of eagles we have vultures and buzzards in the work of God. Instead of people that work in God's house we have people that must be served and its killing revival. Without laser-like focus we will never see God move in our churches again and that's the sad reality of the days we are in.

God commands us to have the mind of Christ and when we do our focus will be on things that really matter and we will experience great moments in our journey with God. When I was young I got a great picture of what laser-like focus was and it has stuck with me to this very day.

I'll never forget going to the Buick open in the year 2000 and watching the greatest golfer who ever lived prepare to win the golf tournament. All the golfers were amazing but this golfer was head and shoulders above the rest. While the other golfers signed autographs, greeted fans, and laughed with others, this golfer was focused completely on the prize ahead of him and nothing was going to stop him.

His focus was off the charts and the announcers said that you couldn't get inside his head with a jackhammer. Other players hated him, said he was rude, and complained about him to the media but he ignored all of that and won more than anyone of his day. Through focus this golfer did things no one else could do and set records that may never be broken.

When we have laser-like focus nothing can stop us and the sad truth is that many stop themselves. If our churches could get people to regain their focus again the gates of Hell could not prevail against us. An eagle is a champion because he refuses to lose focus. Many are losers because they allow everything to rob them of their focus. May God help us all to focus on what's important and ignore things that won't matter in the end.

Anthony Ritthaler

CHAPTER 4:

To Be an Eagle Christian You Must Be a Hard Worker

One of the greatest testimonies that an eagle displays to the world is the testimony of hard work. Whenever you view an eagle in action you will most likely view them giving maximum effort. As soon as the sun comes up an eagle is ready to labor until the sun goes down. All throughout the eagles day he is building, watching, teaching, planning, providing, protecting, hunting, flying, working, fighting, and living life to the fullest.

Something inside of an eagle tells them to be "go getters" and work for everything they have. A man once said, you will never see an out of shape eagle in flight. Eagles do not have a lazy bone in their body and they are successful in life largely due to out working others.

In God's blessed Word you will not find anyone blessed by God who was lazy. The Bible often condemns laziness and says if a man doesn't work he shouldn't eat. God will not bless anyone who refuses to work and to advance in the work of God is impossible without hard labor. Proverbs 20:4 proclaims, "The sluggard will not plow by reason of the cold: therefore shall he beg in harvest, and have nothing."

When we study history, sports, life, and the Bible we find people who made it to the top through dedication and hard work. What you never find is people who made it to the top who wouldn't put in the effort. An author once said this, "Those at the top of the mountain didn't

21

fall there." You will never soar with God on accident, but rather you soar with God with his help and the Bible is clear, hard work is essentially the wings to make that happen.

When you study Olympians and how they train for the Olympics it is an example of how to get to the top. Most athletes training for the Olympics will train anywhere from 12-16 hours a day for 4 years. They train their minds to be disciplined, bodies to be in shape, and their skills to be finely tuned in order to have any shot at the gold medal.

As Christians, God has designed for His children to work hard to accomplish the work of God. If we want to be successful for the Lord, we must strive after hard work all the days of our life. I Corinthians 15:58 says, "Therefore, my beloved brethren, be ye steadfast, unmoveable, always abounding in the work of the Lord, forasmuch as ye know that your labour is not in vain in the Lord."

The Bible promises that if we put in the effort one blessed day we will be rewarded for it. In order to have eagle Christianity and blessings from above we must travel the road paved by hard work. Gordan B. Hinckley said, "Without hard work, nothing grows but weeds."

I've never seen anyone who had God's touch who was lazy, but I've seen many who have the Midas touch because of hard work, and everything they touch turns to Gold spiritually. You cannot just sit in the nest and hope success shows up on your front porch, it doesn't work like that. You must leave the nest and go after what you want in life.

A great man once said, "A dream doesn't become reality through magic; it takes sweat, determination, and hard work. John C. Maxwell said, "Dreams don't work unless you do." From sun up to sun down we should make every second count. The eagle is respected by all and it leads by example in everything it does.

If we want to be successful we cannot skip over labor for God because we are created to work. The Bible says in Ephesians 2:10, "For we are His workmanship, created in Christ Jesus unto good works, which God hath before ordained that we should walk in them."

Jesus said in Luke 9:62, "No man having put his hand to the plough, and looking back is fit for the kingdom of God." In these last days work almost seems like a four letter word to most but if you work, it will result in two four letter words spiritually, "Pure Gold." You will never make it to the palace of the king without laboring at His feet first.

Those who bypass work is like a bird with no wings and eagle Christianity will never be a reality. God's hand is upon an eagle and it can be upon us as well if we follow their pattern. Teddy Roosevelt said, "I would rather risk wearing out than rusting out." An unknown author once said, "You can't have a million dollar dream on a minimum wage work ethic." Allow hard work to carry you to your dreams.

An eagle's testimony screams out to the world hard work and its success is directly connected to it. Let me close out the chapter with this quote, "Who you are tomorrow begins with what you do today." So let's get busy everyone.

Anthony Ritthaler

CHAPTER 5:

You will Never Get to Eagle Christianity without Toughness

When you look up the word tough in the dictionary a picture of a bald eagle may be staring back at you. Everything about an eagle is bad to the bone, and they are tough both physically and mentally. All other birds know that if they mess with an eagle or their young they have an uphill battle they most likely will lose. An eagle looks mean, fights hard, and not only talks the talk but walks the walk.

God has made the eagle one of a kind in the animal kingdom and many don't like eagles but all respect them. Eagles can weather any storm, they are warriors and others will not scare them from accomplishing things they want to accomplish. The quality of toughness has been given to them by God Almighty and they are viewed as champions and winners because they will fight for things they believe in.

As Christians, God wants us to examine the eagles and add toughness to our everyday life. In these last days people are dropping like flies in God's work and it's because everything offends them and they choose the easy road rather than the tough road that leads to power.

I've been humbled and blessed to be around eagle Christians that have experienced God's favor through determination, grit, and a never give up attitude. Weakness has never built a nation or a church but tough minded people sure have. Let me list a handful of people who have inspired me through there toughness and I pray that God will raise up many more just like them.

When I think of eagle toughness I think of men like Dr. Lawrence Mendez, pastor of Open Door Baptist Church in Detroit, Michigan. Dr. Mendez was saved from the rough streets of Detroit and toughness was instilled in him all his life. When he got saved he had a heavy burden to reach his dad but when he visited his dad to tell him about Jesus Christ his own father threw him through a screen door.

Dr. Mendez refused to quit and later won his dad to Jesus and they came as close as close could be. One day his dad grew sick and the family was called to say their last good byes. His father passed away and Dr. Mendez preached his funeral. Although Dr. Mendez loved his dad very much he preached like a wild man that day and after services were over he drove 2 hours to preach at a college and he preached like nothing ever happened. Most would have been sidelined for a while but God gave him the grace to go on and he has never missed a beat.

When I think of eagle toughness my grandfather comes to mind. He had both legs amputated, one eye removed and more health problems that I could list but he rarely ever complained. He was faithful to God's house and loved his Savior and was a light to a dying world. I'll never forget one time my father and I visited him and as he was having a mild heart attack he was telling the doctors about Jesus.

When I think about eagle toughness I think of a dear couple from Hillsdale, Michigan who have been a pastor and pastor's wife for 45 years. Through the years they have both had serious health problems including cancer, diabetes, many surgeries, back problems, heart problems, death of friends and family, trials, heartaches, pain, heartbreak, brain cancer and other major obstacles. Every time I see them they are joyful, friendly, Godly and a blessing. Nothing stops them and toughness defines this dear couple.

When I think of toughness I think of Mr. Dale Roy. Mr. Roy is 90 years old and he reminds me of the modern day Job. In his life he has had mountain top moments but also moments of great pain and valley experiences. Dale has lost three children to death and his only son, Mark, fell out of a tree when he was young and broke his back. Dale was married 66 years to his dear wife, Emma, before he lost her a few years ago.

Dale fought in the war with his brothers and he seen friends die and other horrific things that he won't mention. His kidneys have failed, but God has touched him, bad health at times but God has always helped him through. Dale has seen everything in life and he still has excitement to be in God's house. Dale is a shining light for God and is a blessing to all.

When I think of toughness a preacher from Tennessee comes to mind. This preacher preached 16,000 times without missing a preaching assignment. He has driven over 4 million miles with his 4 kids, and his dear wife and they support 44 missionaries. He has preached through death threats, pain, sickness, overwhelming pressure, and attacks from Satan, yet he refused to stop. That my friends is eagle toughness.

When I think of toughness Deacon Rick Leach jumps out to me. He was saved form the bars and being a bouncer and has become a great servant of God. For years Parkinson's disease has caused him to shake and tremble but his wife would dress him and he would never miss church. Faithful is his middle name and he is the greatest deacon I've ever been around.

When I think of toughness I think of John and Charles Wesley. In their life's they suffered untold afflictions, battles, weariness, hardships, and times of testing but they passed with flying colors. Together they wrote thousands of songs, preached thousands of sermons, seen thousands saved while traveling thousands of miles on horseback in horrible conditions. The devil did everything in his power to try to stop them but they were eagles and they flew for God's glory.

Toughness is lacking in our churches and its hurting the cause of Christ. Ask yourself how tough are you for Christ? Can Jesus count on you to stand strong? Or do you quit when the pressure gets too much?

Jesus expects us to endure hardness as a good soldier and if we do the battle of life can be won. Jesus commanded us to carry our cross daily and we will never be his disciple if we ignore that command. God will only use those who do his commandments and follow in his ways.

Jesus showed us by example how to carry a cross and His love for us drove Him to Calvary. Charles Hadden Spurgeon said and I quote, "No one will wear a crown in heaven, that didn't carry a cross on Earth." Heaven will be filled with eagle Christians from yester year that suffered the lonely life to obtain the crown of righteousness.

The martyrs will be there with a special seat at the table. The disciples who gave their life for the gospels sake will be close to the master at the table. The missionaries, pastors, and servants who fought the good fight of faith will be nearby. Those who were tough will enjoy the fellowship of Christ but I fear many will see Jesus from afar off at the great marriage supper of the Lamb. Oh they will make it thanks to God's grace but they will be in the nose bleed section spiritually speaking and will regret not giving it all to Jesus.

An old preacher once said, "The old time songwriters weren't laying on the beaches of Hawaii drinking lemonade and enjoying the sunshine but they lived the forsaken life, lost everything near and dear to them to bring us the greatest songs ever penned." The Bible says "They that live Godly in Christ Jesus shall suffer persecution." John the beloved brought us the book of Revelation from the lonely isle of Patmos with his eyes poked out.

God uses those who will pay the price for Him and those who have scars from the war. Alexander the Great once came in from the heat of battle and when he stepped in the room all stood at attention. As he looked across the room he seen two men enjoying the party but he noticed they were not like the others. He walked up to them and said young men let me see your scars. They hung their heads and said sir we don't have any. Alexander the Great was enraged and grabbed the two men and removed them from the celebration. Alexander looked at the crowd and said no one should be able to enjoy the party without having scars form the battle.

Heaven will have those who were eagles and those who were pigeons. Folks one day heaven will reveal who was tough and who was weak and some will stand tall and some will be small. I'm thankful for this quote, "Most super heroes wear a cape, but mine wore a cross."

If you are tough you will be an eagle and victory will follow you everywhere you go. Paul said this in II Timothy 4:6-8, "For I am now ready to be offered, and the time of my departure is at hand. I have fought a good fight, I have finished my course, I have kept the faith. Henceforth there is laid up for me a crown of righteousness, which the righteous judge, shall give me at the day: and not to me only, but unto all them also that love his appearing."

Crowns of glory and honor comes to those who are tough in their walk with God. May God give us more toughness in the work of God, and may our feeble efforts bring honor to His holy name. Strive to be tough and your wings will come.

CHAPTER 6:

Without a Fearless Spirit it's Impossible to Have Eagle Christianity

Within the heart of every eagle God created lies a fearless spirit. An eagle is constantly pushing the boundaries, attempting the impossible, and facing every obstacle head on. God has instilled a fire in every eagle's belly to be fearless, and to fly in total faith all his days.

As we watch eagles live we clearly see what God has intended for every child of God through their example of faith, courage, and freedom. Eagles are the intimidators not the intimidated and if we could understand this truth as Christians, we could see a revival like never before. II Timothy 1:7 says, "God hath not given us the spirit of fear, but of power and of love, and of a sound mind."

Christians are taught to be timid, quiet, and robotic, while the Bible teaches us to be fearless, confident, and victors in this dark world. We as saints of God need to have a conquering spirit like the eagle does and we need to have it every day. Satan has God's children running with their tail between their legs but eagle Christianity will charge Hell with a squirt gun.

In these cold, last days Pastors all across the world have sold out to a Godless society and they teach their people that having confidence in the Lord is arrogance. They teach that being fearless for God is rebellious. They teach that if someone has boldness in their faith, they're cocky. This teaching is straight out of Hell and it's no wonder the church sits there in fear because leadership teaches us to be weak not strong.

The Bible says that we are more than conquerors through Him that loved us. An eagle still exists today to remind God's children that there is a powerful, majestic, and free Christian experience that awaits all those who hunger after the Lord. When I think of eagle Christianity many come to mind but David in my opinion is a prime example of soaring with God.

While all of Israel, his brethren, and the king looked at Goliath, fear filled their hearts, and fear gripped their minds, and this went on for forty days. The whole world laughed, mocked, and even labeled David as stubborn, naughty, and foolish. But David ignored all of them and stepped up to the giant with absolutely no fear at all. With God on His side and through an eagle like spirit David slew the giant and even cut off his head and carried it around as a testimony and he became an instant legend for God.

Whenever God puts His touch on anyone that person will be bold, confident in God, powerful, spirit filled, and victorious all the days of their life. Only one man walked on the water and it was a fearless man who worried more about hitting a home run than he did striking out. Christians are terrified to do what Peter did in Matthew 14:29 because they are afraid that if they fall the brethren will laugh at them.

Eagle Christianity does not operate through doubt, worry or fear. The other disciples stayed in the boat but Peter refused to miss his opportunity to fly with God. When you study history, sports, and the Bible you will quickly discover that the legends that stand out in others minds are those who were fearless and went after their dreams while those around them played it safe.

An outstanding hall of fame football player once said this about making it to the Hall of Fame and I quote, "What separates the great players from the good players is a fearless spirit. No one walks within the Halls of the Hall of Fame without playing the game with passion, drive, and a fearless attitude, it separates the men from the boys and those who experience immortality are those who left it all on the field without fear of falling. I'm standing here today because I went for it all every game and though I fell at times my victories were far greater than my defeats."

The greatest baseball player who ever lived said this about his career. "I never worried about striking out because I understood that every strikeout brought me closer to my next homerun." We he retired from baseball he was the all-time homerun leader with 714 homeruns and also the all-time strikeout leader with 1330 strikeouts. Ladies and gentlemen, no one remembers his strikeouts but everyone remembers that he was the king of the homeruns.

Eagles are known as the king of the air and the lions of the sky. As Christians we will never have those titles if we live life weak, defeated and full of fear. The greatest golfer who ever lived said this, "I have won more big tournaments than anyone in history and its only because I was fearless on the golf course. When I sensed fear in others I already knew I won the battle because fear causes you to go backwards but belief causes you to be great. When others feared the big stage, I told myself this is my time to shine and I went after it with all I had."

Thomas Edison said, "I have not failed, I've just found 10,000 ways that won't work, many of life's failures are people who did not realize how close they were to success when they gave up." As Christians we have the victory and it's high time we develop the spirit of the eagle and attack this world with supreme confidence in the victory that is in Christ Jesus.

Twelve men turned the world upside down in the book of Acts and every one of them had fearless spirits. Hebrews chapter eleven is commonly known as the "Hall of Faith" chapter. This wonderful chapter is filled with men and women who were at the top of the mountain with God. They made it into the Hall of Faith through faithfulness, boldness, love, zeal, passion, and belief that God could win every battle for them.

In life no one makes it to the top without a fearless attitude, and in our walk with Christ no one becomes a Hall of Famer spiritually speaking without a fearless conquering spirit, it's impossible. An eagle stands as a picture of the spirit filled life and God wants this from all Christians. If an eagle is not flying on the outside he is dying on the inside.

An eagle is born to fly without fear and Christians are meant to do the same thing spiritually. An eagle has been the national symbol for America for over 200 years because it stands for liberty, freedom, and power and if we want to walk with God we must strive after the spirit of the eagle.

As Christians we need backbone again and total faith that eliminates fear. You cannot walk in faith and fear at the same time. I could give a list a mile long of people who accomplished amazing things through a fearless spirit.

Go after you dreams without fear and your wings for God will begin to grow. Be an eagle not a buzzard. Walk in faith every day and if you fly alone so be it. I'll end this chapter with this quote, "Once you become fearless life becomes limitless." Amen and Amen

CHAPTER 7:

Eagle Christians Must Desire New Heights with God

The great songwriter, Johnson Oatmen, wrote a song called "Higher Ground." This wonderful hymn has inspired untold thousands of Christians to take flight in a way that they never had before. When people all around this world watch an eagle take flight something in their inner being screams out, that all things are possible if we believe.

An eagle can reach heights of 15,000 feet and they can soar upward at 65 mph. when an eagle dives it can reach speeds of 200 mph at its peak. Eagles are always pushing the boundaries of possibility and they have flying on their mind constantly. God has placed them upon planet Earth for many reasons but for Christians they are the blue print of what God intends for us to be. When God saves us he creates in us a clean heart and we are a new creature created in Christ Jesus.

God's design for mankind is that they seek wings spiritually that only he can provide. The Bible is full of verses concerning growing in grace and eagles are mentioned thirty-four times in the Bible for a reason. Watching an eagle soar is the pinnacle of what the Christian life is. It's the very thing we all should strive after and every day we should long after it like hidden treasure.

Proverbs 30:18 says, "There are three things which are too wonderful for me, yea, four which I know not." In verse 19 He describes those things and number one is "the way of the eagle in the air." There is a phrase in the song, "Higher Ground", that should be the anthem of Christian's living, and it should be the cry of our hearts. The phrase in this song says this, "Lord, plant my feet on higher ground." No Christian can experience real revival without allowing God to take over their life in a way that will cause them to fly for His glory.

When an eagle soars he is far from fear, doubt, and cares of this life. As Christians these are the very things that keep us from being air born for Christ. Jesus is the same yesterday, today and forever and His power never ceases to exist. If we aren't flying for God it's not His fault, it's ours.

An eagle will shed every weight that may hold them down but sadly Christians hold onto weight of sin that keeps them on the ground. Many great revivals have shocked the world due to people who decided they wanted to reach new heights.

God give us pastors and people who are tired of living in defeat. Whitfield, the great preacher, said the greatest reason revival don't take hold of folks is because dead pastors are preaching to dead people and no one gets help.

We desperately need an uprising of Christians who hunger and thirst after new heights again. Watch how an eagle flies and decide spiritually that you will do what it take to fly with God. Once you do a fresh anointing from above will carry you to heights you have never known before. God wants us all to fly, never settle for anything else.

CHAPTER 8:

If You Want to Have Eagle Christianity You Must Appreciate the Storms

Before a storm ever hits the area an eagle can sense it coming and instead of hiding like other birds it gets excited. Its first reaction is to go to a high point and wait for the wind to come, which in the Bible is a type of the Holy Spirit. When the storm hits, it sets its wings so that the wind will pick it up and lift it above the storm. The wind shoots the eagle up like a rocket and within a matter of moments the eagle is above the storm clouds and avoids any danger while all other birds feel every effect of the storm. During the storm, not a drop of rain hits the eagle and as he is getting closer to God others are crippled with fear. Eagles love storms because it knows the wind will take it higher than it's ever been before. The eagle understands that God sent the storm not to destroy him but rather to bring him closer to the sun. Only eagles have this mindset and because of it they fly higher and higher while everyone else is afraid.

God will never remove storms from our life, but he can take us through them if we allow the wind to do all the work. When storms come don't try to get through them alone, do what the eagle does and yield to the wind. If we keep our eyes on Jesus we will walk on the water with faith, but if we take our eyes off Him we will drown in the waves.

Faith is the victory and the God of the mountain is still God in the valley. If God brought you to it, God can bring you through it. It's impossible to walk in faith and fear at the same time. Eagles look at the storm as an opportunity to shine, not an opportunity to whine. The stronger the storm rages the higher the eagle soars.

What makes an eagle an eagle is his attitude in the storm. An eagle flies toward the storm, not away from it. People love to shout on the mountain and pout in the valley. Eagles use the negatives of the storm to help them fly higher. We will never grow stronger for God when we are overcome with fear. Eagles appreciate and love every storm and they are never closer to God than they will be in the storm.

Eagles prove that storms can be conquered by the wind, faith, and trust in what God can do. Rejoice through your storms and God will carry you on the wings of eagles, to levels you have never been before. Stop using your own energy in the storm because that will only lead to heartache, frustration, failure and an uphill battle. Use God's energy, not yours and you will fly above any storm life throws your way.

Eagles have no fear during the storm, just freedom to soar above their problems. Allow the Lord to develop you in the storm and you will only get stronger and stronger for God.

CHAPTER 9:

To Become an Eagle Christian You Must Develop Patience

The Word of God constantly talks about the importance of having patience, but so many in these last days refuse to add it to their life. To be patient with things on our heart takes great effort and most will not put in the work required. This world is in a hurry to get nowhere fast and if you don't keep up with the crowd you will get run over.

I've never seen such an impatient, greedy and selfish people like the people of this generation. The world, flesh, and the devil will always try to speed life up, but God will always try to slow things down because he wants us to make wise decisions. So many will sell out their future blessings with God for a little bread now and a lack of patience will lead to life of regret. Watching eagles live teaches mankind many wonderful things and patience is one of them.

Eagles always have a plan and direction in there every day life. Eagles are experts at hunting, building, observing, waiting, and carrying, and without patience none of it is possible. Always remember and rehearse statements like this in your mind, "Rome was not built in a day."

In the Christian life we will not have an empire that will last if we do not exercise patience in our walk with God. The Bible teaches that Abraham was 100 and Sari was 90 when Isaac finally came. At the age of 75 God told Abraham that the promised seed would come through His seed and for 25 long years God made Abraham wait.

The Bible teaches that Joseph waited 13 years and went through much pain and affliction until he was advanced to second in command in Egypt. Noah patiently built an ark to the saving of his house for 120 years. God taught him many lessons and in the end Noah escaped judgement and became a greater man.

Patience is like spiritual medicine that we must consume if we want to grow healthier in the service of God. If we refuse to take our medicine we will never grow into mature, strong, and healthy Christians. The Bible commands us to have the patience of Job but many will ignore verses of that nature. Patience does not come natural but we are supposed to add it to our faith and work on it every day.

The Bible says the trial of our faith worketh patience and if we add it to our spiritual life we will grow into something beautiful for God. The majority of mistakes we will make in life will be due to us being in a hurry. Never allow people or your emotions to rush you as you go along your journey.

Eagles do not try to keep up with the new fashions or trends of the day. They don't worry about being popular, nor do they ask for approval to fly. This world is fast pace and if we are not careful we can get caught up competing with others and it leads to stressed out people.

The devil has turned this world into a race toward disaster and people by the untold billions are traveling at record speeds toward a dead end road. One hundred years ago, America seen great revivals and people spent much time with God. Today we spend little time with God and revival for many is a thing of the past.

Eagle Christians will be controlled by the wind, not the world. Add patience to your life and in due season ye shall reap on God's timing not yours.

CHAPTER 10:

To Be an Eagle Christian You Must be Sensitive to the Holy Spirit

Storms will come in every Christian's life and when we are sensitive to the Holy Spirit He will lead us away from danger not towards it. Whenever we grieve the Holy Spirit we lose direction in our lives and we lose that security blanket God offers in the form of protection. When a storm arises in an eagle's life He follows the wind and it carries him away from trouble and into glory.

If there are sudden changes in the weather eagles can sense it because they have their eye on the sun and because they are yielded to the wind of God. Eagles will enjoy the sunshine while others feel the effects of the storm because they keep the wind as a compass in their life at all times.

Many storms in our life could be avoided or handled much easier if we allowed the Spirit of God to guide us instead of us shutting Him out completely. It's vital for all Christians to learn that God has a better way for us and if we trust His leadership it will always lead us to a brighter outcome. Being sensitive to the Holy Ghost will save us from trouble we don't even know exists.

Always remember God sees up the road and knows the outcome before it happens. We don't have that ability so it's important that we grab unto His nail pierced hand and let Him lead. Let me give you a story that will shed a light on the value of being sensitive to the pleading of the Holy Spirit.

A dear man of God went to school to be a pilot and loved flying with all His heart. Every time he got a chance to fly he took advantage of it and patiently learned the ways of the air. To him it was relaxing and a great stress reliever and he spent hours perfecting his craft and he enjoyed every second of it. One morning as he was praying, from out of nowhere Gods sweet Holy Spirit softly spoke to him and he said it was clear as a bell. The Holy Spirit told him to take his pilot license, put it away and never fly again unless He told him too.

The preacher was heartbroken but didn't hesitate and cancelled his flight scheduled for him that afternoon. People thought he was nuts but he knew God spoke to Him and what happened next stunned everyone. A man took his place that day and shortly after reaching the air the plane went down and killed him instantly. Everyone was stunned including the preacher and they didn't think he was nuts anymore. To this day he has never flown again and travels the country every day preaching the gospel of Jesus Christ. Without being sensitive to the Spirit of God he would not be here today and thousands may have never been reached for God.

Every morning we get up we should ask the Spirit of God to nudge us when danger is near. The Holy Spirit can keep us safe at all times and if we are directed by God we will be able to hear His voice leading us towards victory not tragedy. Spend your life drawing closer to God and you will hear his voice when you need it the most.

Yield to the wind and He will lift you to your maximum potential ignore the wind and you may just go down in flames. Thank God for the Holy Ghost who comforts, instructs, and guides us throughout life's way. When God told Noah to build an ark he was laughed at by the world but when the rains pounded the area they changed their minds quickly. Never underestimate the power of God's Spirit and follow His leading and it will benefit you greatly.

Anthony Ritthaler

CHAPTER 11:

If you Desire to be an Eagle Christian You Must Allow God to Renew Your Strength

The most famous verse about eagles in Scripture is found in Isaiah 40:31. You will find it in most Christian stores but many do not comprehend what it really means and how important it is in their own personal walk with God. If we long to have power, longevity, and influence with God we must allow God to make this a reality not just a hope in our walk with the Lord. Here is what the beautiful verse says, "But they that wait upon the Lord shall renew their strength; they shall mount up with wings as eagles: they shall run, and not be weary; they shall walk and faint."

Be honest, when is the last time you felt a fresh anointing and a refreshing spiritual shower of power rush through your soul? For many it's been a very long time, for others it's never happened once and instead of enjoying freedom you're treading water spiritually. God wants us to renew ourselves like the eagle and experience full maturity in Christ that takes us far from duds to studs for God.

When an eagle is born, he is saturated by the sun, surrounded by the father, serenaded by love, sheltered from the storms, and sought after by the wind. These five things stick with him and mature him as he starts to grow. An eaglet is taught how to fly and as he grows he gets stronger and more confident and eventually leaves the nest to start his own journey in life.

At the age of five an eaglet has everything he needs to succeed and stay soaring and he enters full maturity and is on his way to greatness. If I placed a five year old bald eagle next to a thirty-five year old eagle none of us could tell the difference because like the Bible says they renew their strength every day and year in and year out they look the same.

Maturity in Christ will lead us to follow after the same pattern eagles follow and I will list them now. The first way an eagle renews his strength is by spending time with the wind and letting it carry him through life. An eagle when flying only uses his own strength ten percent of the time and uses God's strength (the wind), ninety percent of the time. All other birds flap their wings constantly while flying and because of this they get weary much quicker.

A study was done on a bald eagle in flight and the results were overwhelming. They found that in an hour of flying that eagle used the wind to carry him 58 minutes out of 60 and didn't look tired at all. An eagle understands down deep in his soul that if he wants to remain fresh, strong, and renewed with God he must use the wind as his friend or he will burn out and fall to the world as a failure.

Christians all over this country are falling out of church, giving up hope, and losing the fight because they are trying to serve God with their own strength and without the Holy Spirit's strength. Without yielding to God's power, we will wear out every time and we will end up discouraged in this battle. Yielding to the wind will keep us vibrate, strong, and renewed for God's glory.

May God help us all to follow the eagle's example of yielding to the wind every chance we get. If we do we will feel young, anointed, and victorious as a Christian.

Another way an eagle renews his strength daily is by spending time with the sun. All throughout the day eagles bask in the sun, stare at the sun, and fly towards the sun. The first thing a baby eaglet sees upon being born is the sun and this pattern continues all his life. An eagle allows the sun to protect him, comfort him, and shine upon him daily and it causes a renewing that refreshes him all his life.

If we Christians had this same mindset toward the Son we would be renewed like never before. If you're feeling broken allow the light of God's Son to revive you, restore you, and renew you. All throughout the day think about the son, seek after the son, and run towards the Son and your imprisoned soul will fly for His honor and glory.

Another reason eagles are renewed is because they spend time daily in the air. You see eagles are meant to fly not walk and the more they fly the more renewed with God they feel. The higher the eagle gets the more freedom they experience and the younger their hearts stay.

We, as Christians, need to let go of our chains that bind us and fly as much as possible. Don't let anyone clip your wings, grab onto the hand of faith, let go of the spirit of fear and a refreshing form God will invade your life in a wonderful new way.

The fourth way an eagle renews his strength is by spending his time around the water. For an eagle the water is a major part of his daily life and it renews him over and over again. An eagle will swim in the water, drink the water, get food from the water, refresh himself in the water, and live close to the water. Eagles cannot survive without water and it is a key to his success all his days.

If we desire a renewing with God, the water of the Word must be our source and we must thirst after it day in and day out. The water from above will hydrate our spirit and it will keep us feeling great in our journey with God. We, as humans, cannot go too long without water and if we keep that in mind spiritually we will stay energetic for Jesus.

The last thing eagles make sure they do daily for renewal with God is they spend time with the rock. Eagles carve out time every day to pull out old feathers while leaning on a rock. Eagles pluck out anything that they feel holds them down and makes them feel and look old. They go through a cleansing and an eagle always remembers the rock where it was born at. Eagles know that if they go to the rock and stare at the sun they will stay renewed all the days of their life.

Every time we are overwhelmed and beat down in life we need to run to the rock of our salvation and relief will quickly come. Psalm 61: 2 says, "From the end of the earth will I cry unto thee, when my heart is overwhelmed. Lead me to the rock that is higher than I." All the renewing and refreshing we will ever need is found in the rock of ages.

Eagles stay young, strong, mature, and powerful all their life because they depend on God's ability to renew them, not their own. We must follow this pattern if we want to make a difference in this battle against darkness. Psalm 103:5 says, "Who satisfieth thy mouth with good things; so that thy youth is renewed like the eagles."

Always remember the eagle's pattern; spend time with the wind, the sun, the air, the water, and the rock and you will stay young for God, We will never mount up with wings as eagles without His help. Eagle Christianity keeps us fresh, joyful, excited for God and all other methods will cause us to grow old in a hurry. Thank God there is a renewing that is available to all who hunger after a closer relationship with the Lord.

Anthony Ritthaler

CHAPTER 12:

Eagle Christianity will Always Involve Fullness Of Joy

Nehemiah 8:10 clearly states that the joy of the Lord is our strength and without joy we will always remain weak as Christians. When you study out the life of eagles you discover that they love to soar, and they love to have fun as they live each day. Eagles only spend about 2 hours a day hunting and much of the day they do aerial tricks and they really don't care who it offends. They will spin in the air, do amazing things and they even do cartwheels.

When eagles are going through the dating process or courtship phase they will meet high in the air lock talons and tumble through the sky displaying their love for one another and right before they land they will separate. Eagles show us by their example that when you are in love you will enjoy each other's company and you will do cartwheels in the presence of all. Eagles are the only bird in the world that does cartwheels as they ride the wind through the air.

As Christians we should never be afraid of enjoying our walk with God and every day we should lock arms with the Holy Ghost and do spiritual cartwheels for His glory. Peter said that we should have joy unspeakable and full of glory. Most Christians are miserable, sad, discouraged, depressed, and weak and having joy is the last thing they desire.

There are good people that work hard but are powerless through labor and without assistance from the wind of the Holy Spirit. People who have joy, shine for God and everyone takes notice. We will never have the fruit of the spirit without joy and we will never enjoy life without it either.

Jesus said that he came that we might have life and have it more abundantly. God never wants His children to be cold, bitter, and weary in the battle, but He wants us all to smile, laugh, and dance through His Spirit. Acts 3:7-8 says, "And he took him by the right hand, and lifted him up: and immediately his feet and ankle bones received strength. And he leaping up stood, and walked, and entered with them into the temple, walking, and leaping, and praising God," Ask yourself when is the last time you shouted, worshipped, leaped, danced, and had overflowing joy?

The Bible says when John the Baptist was in his mother's womb he heard of Jesus and he leaped for joy in his mother's womb. Christians all across this planet function without joy and they have no effect on a lost and dying world. When a Christian is endued with power from on high joy will be automatic in his walk with God.

Churches are dead, powerless, lifeless, and feeble because they are not plugged into the glory world and they are weighed down by the cares of life. You will never fly spiritually, carrying baggage of sin, worry, doubt, fear, and heartache around everywhere you travel. You must let go of your problems and allow the wind of the Holy Ghost to do the work for you.

The Bible says, "Where the Spirit of the Lord is there is liberty." Without the wind of joy blowing in our lives this world will never want what we have. God is too great to walk around defeated. Do what the eagle does, fly through the air without a care in the world and the wind will lead you on a journey you will never forget.

Joyful Christians are strong, excited, and free in their walk with the Lord. Once you add joy the impossible becomes possible and the battle will be won through the power of His son. Fall in love with the Savior more and more every day and you too will do a cartwheel for the glory of almighty God.

Anthony Ritthaler

CHAPTER 13:

To Be an Eagle Christian You Must Be a Great Hearer

Although an eagles vision is superior, its hearing is excellent as well. Eagles spend very few time talking, or making noise but it spends a lot of time listening and it greatly helps them achieve greatness. Eagles have this kind of testimony, say little in life and open up your hearing and God will bless you greatly.

God gave us one mouth and two ears for a reason and if we understand that we will be better in our walk with God. When I was young and struggling in my Christian life, God led me to buy 140 CDs of preaching and I grew more in those 3 months then in all my previous 30 years combined. In 3 months I heard over 200 sermons and did not say a word. God's power filled my heart on several occasions and faith will always come by hearing and hearing by the word of God.

Many around this country love to talk but very few love to listen and we will never be effective in a one way conversation. We must be like a sponge if we want to learn the ways of the eagle. The eagle is always alert, always awake, and always listening in order to be successful. James 1:19 says, "Wherefore, my beloved brethren, let every man be swift to hear, slow to speak, slow to wrath."

Jesus said he that hath ears to hear let him hear. The best thing you can ever do as a Christian is to grab your Bible, lock yourself in a room with a stack of Godly music and preaching cd's and don't come out until you're filled to overflowing with God's power. Be like the eagle, listen, focus, love the meat and God will lead you to the water that will refresh your hurting soul.

We need more people to be tuned in to God and many of the problems they tell everyone about will start to fade away. A man once said, "The quieter you become, the more you can hear." And that's always the case with God. Those who listen far more than they talk will always have the potential to be eagle like.

My advice to all believers is when you come into church gear your mind to hear God's voice and He may just bid you to fly. The art of hearing is missing in these last days and an eagle's testimony encourages all to listen more than running your mouth and great things will happen. A great man once said, "Don't quack like a duck, soar like an eagle."

Many talk a big game but when it comes time to fly they are just filled with hot air. Someone once said, "You cannot soar with eagles if you're hanging around turkeys." Be careful who you hang with because talkers can clip your wings and keep you from taking off for God. Listen more than you talk and God will always send the wind for you.

CHAPTER 14:

If We Want Eagle Christianity We Must Go After Wisdom From Above

A famous leader once said this quote and I pray we never forget it, "In an eagle is all the wisdom of the world." When God created an eagle he created wisdom and power in motion. Eagles were created with incredible gifts and one of those gifts is wisdom from on high. God longs for mankind to observe the eagle not ignore it.

We could spend a lifetime studying a bald eagle's wisdom but we would be just scratching the surface. Eagles prepare like no other, fly like no other, and it all looks effortless. The eagle is wise in building, choosing a mate, eating, sleeping, taking care of family, hunting, protecting, refreshing, and living to its greatest potential.

The way the eagle moves, glides, and operates is different than others because of its wisdom of the wind, and it avoids trouble others fly right into. The eagles greatest advantage over their enemies is the ability to use God's strength in battle not their own. An eagle's wisdom will carry him through life and allow him to make smart choices for the glory of God.

The Bible says that wisdom is far better than rubies and diamonds and if you want to be a jewel for God you must have great wisdom. Solomon could have wanted anything from God but when he chose wisdom God was happy and gave him not only wisdom but also all the riches life had to offer.

Those who go after God's wisdom will be carried by the wind all their life and the Lord will increase their success rate for Him. The Bible says in Daniel 1:20 that four young men had ten times more wisdom and understanding than all the magicians and astrologers of that time and as a result they advanced for God every day.

Man's wisdom on its best day is no match for God's on his worst day and what's great about that is God never has an off day. Gipsy Smith said, "I would rather obtain wisdom at Jesus' feet than to hold every degree of every secular college in the world at one time."

Eagles are a cut above the rest because they use wisdom in everything they do. Many are going after education of man and their getting smarter by the world's standards but they can't fly with the Lord and they don't understand why. Folks without wisdom from above we will never have power to soar.

Some of the greatest preachers I've ever been around were those who never went to school but spent hours a day learning at the master's feet. Paul said that his preaching was not with enticing words of man's wisdom, but in demonstration of the spirit and of power. God wants us to have ministries that man can't explain not ones that man can explain.

The eagle soars above the clouds and they leave everyone wondering how. The Bible says in James that wisdom that descendeth not from above, is earthly, sensual, devilish speaking of man's wisdom. Preachers all over this country look good, smell good, speak well, have large followings, but the power of God is a thousand miles away. We need preachers that study and know what it's like to fly again in America.

James 3:17 says, But the wisdom that is from above is first pure, then peaceable, gentle, and easy to be entreated, full of mercy, and good fruits, without partiality, and without hypocrisy." Man's wisdom deals with the mind and people love that because it doesn't offend them and they walk away feeling good but never growing. God's wisdom deals with a man's heart, and we may not like it but it is spiritual medicine that heals the soul.

Those who hunger after wisdom from above will always be successful in God's work, those who won't hunger after it will always watch others fly but never will themselves. Wisdom is available to all and James 1:5 says, "If any man lack wisdom, let him ask of God, that giveth to all men liberally, and upbraideth not, and it shall be given him."

Jesus said we have not because we ask not. If we really want eagle Christianity wisdom is a must. Proverbs 3:5-6 says, "Trust in the Lord with all thine heart, and lean not unto thine own understanding. In all thy ways acknowledge him, and he shall direct thy paths." The eagle teaches us that if we forsake doing things in our own power and lean on the strength of the wind, wisdom will take over and carry us right to God's throne.

Anthony Ritthaler

CHAPTER 15:

Eagle Christianity Comes Easier when you Honor You Father and Mother

I've never in my life seen anyone flourish who disrespected their parents but for 36 years I've seen many cursed by the hand of God for doing so. There is great blessings in honoring your parents and there are severe judgments to those who rebel. I've never heard Proverbs 30:17 preached on in church but this is what it says, "The eye that mocketh at his father, and despiseth to obey his mother, the ravens of the valley shall pick it out, and the young eagles shall eat it." That verse is very serious and when you don't honor the parents God gave you, judgment, misery, and pain will always hover over you like a dark cloud.

The Bible is clear that it's a uphill climb to any and all who makes foolish choices in their youth and spiritual crumbs is all they will enjoy if there are any at all. In the Old Testament the Bible says whoso curseth the father and mother let him die the death. Proverbs 20:20 says, "Whoso curseth father or his mother, his lamp shall be put out in obscure darkness."

Folks when God turns the light off He has no intention of turning it back on. Many adults are under the curse of God as I write because they were rebels in their young days and God turned them off. On the other hand, there are amazing benefits, rewards, blessings, and power that comes with honoring mom and dad.

First of all there is long life according to the old and New Testament. Secondly there is favor with the

Lord that will lift you and elevate you to heights others will never know. Last of all, God will smile down upon your life and give you wings to soar and your cup will overflow for Gods glory.

Psalm 23: 6 says, "Surely goodness and mercy shall follow me all the days of my life: and I will dwell in the house of the Lord forever." I'm thankful that God has given me such great parents and all my life I've tried to honor them and God has opened up Heaven and poured out blessings because of it.

Eagles are fierce, serious, and warriors, but they are also providers, tender and great teachers. The eagle loves their children and is always spending time with them, and investing in them. If the eaglet has the right attitude eventually it will have the chance to fly. However, if it is does not heed the lessons taught by mom and dad it will not fly and it will never survive.

The eagle who listens will do cartwheels for God one day but if they do not they will never experience what flying is all about. If your mom and dad are still around hug them, kiss them, and get things right and maybe one day you will leave the ground and take to the air. People who try to fly that have broken relationships with their parents will miserably fail.

You can move from an eaglet to an eagle if you obey your parents if you refuse you will always be a spiritual baby with no wind beneath your wings.

CHAPTER 16:

Eagle Christians Will Always Use Their Time Wisely

When you study an eagles sleep patterns and way of living you will find it produces success and victory and it's a pattern we all should follow. All eagles have balance, discipline, and structure in their lives and very little time is ever wasted and productivity is always at work in their lives. Eagles will go to sleep right when the sun goes down and get up right when the sun comes up and repeat the same pattern every day.

An eagle will use its time wisely during the day and they will squeeze everything they can out of the day when there is light. Eagles won't sleep half the day away, and they won't wait to the end of the day to accomplish things. Time is always precious to an eagle and they are all about using their time wisely and living life to the fullest.

Christians and people in general desperately need to wake up out of their wasteful patterns and make their life count for God. The Bible says in Ephesians 5:16, "Redeeming the time, because the days are evil." We are commanded to use our time wisely and the majority of the world is ignoring this verse.

The Bible implores us to wake up out of our sleep walking and we need to get back to seeking after God not the newest fade or fashion. The devil has this world blinded like never before and precious time is slipping away. Statistics tell us that the average person sleeps 8.8 hours a day and the average teen plays electronics of some kind around 9 hours a day. If that's not bad enough the average adult reads 19 minutes a day while the average teen about 9 minutes a day.

Satan has provided entertainment for all and people eat it up like candy but it leaves people empty, void, and unproductive in life. As long as people play games for 9 hours a day and read for 9 minutes, society will go downhill and we will continue to be a mess. Satan is slick and he is a master at stealing people's time and future and he has a strong hold on people's minds and hearts.

Eagles refuse to allow anyone or anything to stop productivity and we should do the same thing. Good people are wrapped up in fun, entertainment, sports, pleasure, and wasteful living and God's heart breaks for them. God designed man to walk with him in the cool of the day and to spend time walking with Him

If we wake up every morning seeking fellowship with the master joy will be a major part of our life and we will affect others for the work of God. Jesus said this in Luke 9:62, "No man having put his hand to the plough, and looking back, is fit for the kingdom of God." As long as we allow everything to stop us from moving forward for God we will not be pleasing to our great Lord.

When Lot's wife looked back she was turned into a pillar of salt and she sold out her future blessings with God. Christians we need to settle it in our hearts that our time will be used wisely and we will build a kingdom for God. We cannot feed our flesh more than our spirit and expect to go anywhere great. As long as we reject God, waste time, and throw the best years of our lives away we will be a train wreck spiritually.

Eagles are the masters of the air and they are great examples of hard work, determination, and spending their time wisely. Let's get busy for the Lord and let's be eagles for the Savior. Make every second count and always be active for the Lord and you will have a legacy all your own.

CHAPTER 17:

If you long for Eagle Christianity you can't Allow Others to Rob You of Your Freedom

Jesus said, "If the son therefore shall make you free, ye shall be free indeed." But many in our churches live in bondage every day. When Jesus saved us He set us free from the spirit of fear and He gives all His children the ability to fly. II Timothy 1:7 says this, "For God hath not given us the spirit of fear, but the power, and of love, and of a sound mind." If we aren't flying high for the Lord it's not God's fault it's our own.

Many Christians live in the past mistakes they made and they allow others to hang it over their head but let me boldly say your past is forgotten, cast into the deepest sea. Galatians 5:1 says, "Stand fast in the liberty wherewith Christ hath made us free, and be not entangled again with the yoke of bondage." In church Christians hang their head and know nothing about liberty available through the power of the Holy Ghost.

Eagles fly without permission from others and they enjoy every second of it. Where are the saints that spread their wings and fly above their problems? You cannot soar with fear in your heart, it just doesn't work like that. The Bible teaches that the fear of the man bringeth a snare. Many fear man and allow their judgmental spirit to dictate their flight for God.

Child of God with the help of the wind we can soar to levels with God the Pharisees will never know. Far too many people can't get past mistakes they have made and because of it they stay defeated and in chains of depression. Always remember if God can set free a man with 6000 demons and cause him to fly spiritually, He can cause you to fly too.

There are more books about joy than ever recorded but less people have joy than ever before. Don't allow Satan to keep you Earthbound/ if you are struggling to fly allow God to renew you today. I John 3:8 says, "He that committeth sin is of the devil: for the devil sinneth from the beginning, for this purpose the son of God was manifested, that he might destroy the works of the devil."

John 10:10 clearly says, "I am come that they might have life, and that they might have it more abundantly." If you know the Lord there is no reason you should remain helpless and weak spiritually. Go to His throne boldly and you will find grace to help in your time of need. An eagle in flight is God's way to convey to His children that there is freedom to all who yield their life to His Will. Don't settle for the average and don't allow guilt to control you anymore.

If you want to soar it's up to you. We need more saints of God to realize that God's plan for them is to reach new heights. Soar without fear and God will carry you towards new victory and fresh freedom in Christ.

John 8:36 says, "So if the son sets you free, you are free indeed." Freedom should be our motto not fear, be an eagle and don't let anyone rob you of your liberty with the Lord.

CHAPTER 18:

To Have Eagle Christianity We Must be Swift and Think One Step Ahead

David is mentioned in God's Word over and over and over again and he was and always will be a man after God's own heart. David's wisdom was vast and his influence is unmatched so when he speaks we should all pay close attention.

In II Samuel 1:23 he was honoring two men that made an impact on him and revealing to us how we should live if we want to make a difference for God. II Samuel 1:23 says this, "Saul and Jonathan were lovely and pleasant in their lives, and in their death they were not divided they were swifter than eagles, they were stronger than lions." In this verse David wanted to honor men with these qualities and he is saying through God's spirit that if we as Christians have these same qualities we will impact all around us.

If you study out the eagle most of everything it accomplishes is through swift speed and swift thinking. The eagle is not only powerful, fast and wise, but it is also thinking one step ahead of others and its success rate is off the charts. They say an eagle hits its prey with twice the force of a rifle bullet. They can dive at nearly two hundred mph and can see fish under the water from several hundred feet away. Eagles don't waste their talents and gifts that God has given them and they go after it without delay.

Christians all over this world are missing out on great things God has for them because instead of being swift when God deals with them they allow Satan to convince them to wait. When you're an eagle Christian you react quickly to the voice of God and you do not delay. If God deals with you about teaching, you do it. If God deals with you about giving, you should say yes Lord. If God tells you to help others, you do it quickly. If God tells you to visit someone, you act swiftly.

Whatever He deals with us about we must do it swiftly if we want to reach our maximum flight with God. We will never grow to eagle status until we stop allowing Satan to change our minds concerning things God wants us to do. God blesses those who act swiftly in the work of God.

An old missionary once said that every time God speaks to you and you say yes to His will the next time He speaks His voice gets clearer, but everything you say no to His voice and delay, His voice gets softer and softer to the point of you not hearing it at all. God has a great future laid out for all of us, but he can't make decisions for us. The devil will always try to get you to act in doubt not faith. If the devil can convince you to wait just one more day that day will turn into years and you will look back later in life and regret that you didn't respond immediately to God's voice. Great blessings and peace are given to those who respond swiftly to God's voice and they are always fruitful in their life.

When an eagle sees an opportunity to shine he doesn't play around and say I'll do it tomorrow, he reacts swiftly and attacks whatever he is going after. As Christians we need to start doing God's Will today because tomorrow may never come. So many will miss out on being great because they choose to listen to Satan instead of God.

Wake up early every morning seeking God's will and stop avoiding it and eagle Christianity will take over your life. React swiftly to God's voice and He will lead you into new realms of power, react slowly to His voice and you may miss out on everything altogether. Eagles will always be overcomers and winners because they refuse to allow anything to stop them from flying and going after things they desire.

Let us learn to be swift in our decisions for God and the Lord will bless us with fresh meat form above every day. Isaiah 1:19-20 says this, "If ye be willing and obedient, ye shall eat the good of the land: but if ye refuse and rebel, ye shall be devoured with the sword: for the mouth of the Lord hath spoken it." What separates eagle Christians from buzzard Christians is obedience to Gods voice and saying yes in a timely fashion.

Don't miss out on blessing from above, be swift like the eagle and you will glide through life spiritually. Think a step ahead of others and have an urgency about decisions for God and you will move to the front of the class for God.

CHAPTER 19:

To Be an Eagle Christian You Must Be a Meat Eater

God has put into the heart and mind of eagles to go after one thing and this is meat. Nothing else interests or satisfies their taste buds and when they go after meat they do it with passion, zeal, and hunger. In the morning they are not going after cereal, pop tarts, or donuts but rather strong meat. At dinner it's not fat, junk and things that make them weak, but its meat, meat and more meat. All hours of the day consist of fish, protein, small animals, and meat at all times. An eagle is able to hold up to two pounds of fish in their belly at one time. They love meat, they desire meat, and they never get tired of it and never complain about it.

An expert once said, you will never see an out of shape eagle in flight. Eagles don't need a variety of different food. They just need meat to make it through each day. The bald eagle is the king of the air because he is strong, confident, healthy and eating the proper thing to help him grow to his maximum ability.

Most Christians I know go after everything except strong meat and they stagger around like spiritual zombies, weak, cold, stiff, frail, and Earth bound all the days of their life. Paul rebuked the church for only drinking the milk of the Word and rejecting the meat. Paul was an eagle and he gave his life to feed them the meat but they refused it and only grew worse.

The apostle Paul was flying with power while the people he loved were dying spiritually. In these last days we don't have eagles who live on meat. We have leeches that suck the blood out of the body. In these last days people don't hunger after the meat of the Word anymore but rather feast on junk that makes them sick spiritually. It doesn't matter how many plays, skits, games, programs, entertainment, rock bands, smoke, dinners on the ground, fleshly activities, or social clubs we take in. without meat from above we will never grow for the cause of Christ.

We, like the eagle, need to be hungry for the meat and if the meat of God's Word is gone from the pulpit we better go to somewhere it exists. All Christians should desire 100% meat at all times and never take things into our spiritual system that makes us sick, weak, powerless, and useless for God.

Hebrews 5:12-14 says this, "For when for the time ye ought to be teachers, ye have need that one teach you again which be the first principles of the oracles of God; and are become such as have need of milk and not strong meat. For every one that useth milk is unskillful in the word of righteousness: for he is a babe. But strong meat belongeth to them that are full age, even those who by reason of use have their senses exercised to discern both good and evil."

The word of God clearly declares in these verses that without strong meat we will always be babes feeding on the milk and we will have no discernment and direction in life. Most Christians we talk to don't know the Bible but they know about everything else and it's killing our churches.

In our spiritual diets we need to forsake everything else and desire the meat of God's Word if we want to grow strong for the Lord. Wake up each morning saying.

"God feed me meat," and the power from above will be manifested in your daily life. Flying is impossible without a steady diet of meat and victory is absent to anyone who doesn't feed their spirit more than their flesh.

Nothing in this world is more important for the nourishment of the soul than the meat of God's Word. We can do without a bunch of things in church but meat is not one of them. Be an eagle and live for the meat and you will be healthy, flourishing, and majestic for God's glory.

CHAPTER 20:

If You Want to Have Eagle Christianity, Fly Towards the Sun

When an eagle is born, it is born with three lens built into its eyes that protect them all the days of their life. They basically have sunglasses built into their eyes that helps them look directly into the sun and even fly towards the sun without any harm and their enemies can't handle it.

One of the biggest enemies to eagles are crows because they know if they attach onto their back, the eagle can't do anything to defend itself because of its size. When this happens an eagle waits for the wind current to pick up and it lets off a scream and takes off towards the sun at an incredible speed. As the eagle gets higher the lens kick in and the sun doesn't hurt them but rather helps them destroy the enemy, which is a type of flesh. The higher the eagle gets the more it hurts the crow and eventually the enemy loses its grip and falls to the ground.

All of the eagles life it flies towards the sun and the higher it flies the more freedom it experiences. God has blessed eagles with this gift, physically to show us the secret of life spiritually.

Whenever we are in trouble we need to stop running towards man's method, drugs, alcohol, doctors, shrinks, medicine, or whatever else offers quick fixes but no relief. Do what the eagle does and fly directly towards the sun and we can experience permit victory in our Christian walk with the Lord. Hebrews 12:2 says

"Looking unto Jesus the author and finisher of our faith." The Bible says "If the son therefore shall make you free, ye shall be free indeed."

Millions all across this world could have freedom if they would realize that all victory is found in flying towards the son, not going to quick fixes. The Son of God can melt away all fears we have and never forget there is healing in His wings. Far too many people are drowning daily in an ocean of fear, but the eagle flies in freedom through the wings provided by God.

When we make our way towards the Son of God, life will become brighter and we will burn hotter for God's glory. We need to swallow our pride and allow the Son to fight our battles for us. The devil loves to apply the heat on his level but when we apply the heat through the Son of God he will eventually flee from us.

An eagle will take a snake by the throat and carry it to the air. When they get up in the air it chokes the snake and it is no match for the eagle. Far too many fight Satan on the ground through the flesh and the devil keeps them captive at his own will. Successful Christians will always fight Satan through God's spirit because that's the only way victory is possible. Galatians 5:16 says this "Walk in the spirit, and ye shall not fulfil the lust of the flesh." The Bible also declares that where the spirit of the Lord is there is liberty.

Every battle won in life will be through the Son, and an eagle uses this truth to his advantage. An eagle is never ashamed or afraid to fly towards the sun and if we want to triumph over the enemy we must do the same thing.

Romans 16:20 says "And the God of the peace shall bruise Satan under your feet shortly." May this wonderful verse be the testimony of all of our lives'. An eagle will strike great fear in its enemy through its power, strength and conquering spirit.

If we want to be an eagle spiritually, we must stop being controlled by fear and we must fly towards the sun all the days of our life. Ephesians 5:14 says "Wherefore he saith, awake then that sleepest, and arise from the dead, and Christ shall give thee light." The brighter the Son shines in our life the more the devil will hide in fear.

Malachi 4:2 says, "But unto you that fear His name shall the son of righteousness arise with healing in his wings." There is great healing in the Son and with Gods help we can be spiritually healthy and vibrant every day. Most Christians live in fear but eagles live with total faith and this is why we are weak and they are strong. Thank God for the Son of God who protects us from all danger. Run towards the sun and your wings will come.

Anthony Ritthaler

CHAPTER 21:

To Experience Eagle Christianity You Must Love the Water

All throughout God's' blessed book you will find that water is comparable to the word and moving water is comparable to the Holy Spirit. Eagles surround themselves with water and they always build their nest within shouting distance of water. An eagle spends time daily viewing water, drinking water, hunting by the water, and yes eagles enjoy swimming in the water too.

Water is important part of the eagle's life and without it they cannot function the same nor can they survive. God has designed eagles to always go after water and if we are born again he has designed us to long after water as well. Isaiah 55:1 says, "Ho, every one that thirsteth, come ye to the waters, and he that hath no money; come ye, buy, and eat; yea, come, buy wine and milk without money and without price."

David said this in Psalm 42:1-2, "As the hart panteth after the water brooks, so panteth my soul after thee, O God. My soul thirsteth for God, for the living God: when shall I come and appear before God?" As Christians something inside us should be thirsty for the water from above and if we are not thirsty something is wrong.

Salvation gets sweeter every day for those who allow God to satisfy them with the water of the Word. Eagles always have an eye on the water and will visit it all throughout His life. If we want to enjoy life and stay hydrated for His glory we must thirst after water and let it restore our souls.

Psalm 23 is the most famous chapter at funerals but in all honesty it's a chapter for the living who want to soar with God. Psalm 23: 1-3 says this, "The Lord is my shepherd; I shall not want. He maketh me to lie down in green pastures: He leadeth me beside still waters. He restoreth my soul: he leadeth me in the paths of righteousness for his name sake." Saint of God if we will keep life simple and go to the water as much as possible we will find rest, comfort, and refreshing that the world cannot offer.

People all around this planet stray from the narrow path that leads to eternal water and travel towards destruction and danger and it will destroy them. The water that this world gives will leave your soul barren, dry, and empty but the water Jesus offers will always fill the thirsty soul. John 4:13-14 says this, "Jesus answered and said unto her, whosoever drinketh of this water shall thirst again. But whosoever drinketh of the water that I shall give him shall never thirst: but the water that I shall give him shall be in him a well of water springing up into everlasting life."

Nothing Satan offers will ever satisfy the hurting soul but Jesus has the never ending supply that will keep us content and happy. We must stay close to the water of the Word, if we do not we will lose our strength and dry up on God. No Christian can make it without a healthy supply of God's water.

As an eagle longs for it physically we must long for it spiritually or we will end up a failure somewhere down life's road. A famous person once said, "If there is magic on this planet, it is contained in water." Child of God I'm here to tell you there is magic in God's Word and the more you use it and drink it the more you will see miracles take place.

Those who frequently use and partake in the water of the Word will fly higher and higher for God. God's water is free but its value goes beyond what money can buy. Revelation 22:17 says this, "And the spirit and the bride say, come, and let him that is athirst come, and whosoever will let him take of the water of life freely." Allow God's water to refresh you, revive you, and restore you and like the eagle you will experience freedom that goes beyond human comprehension.

CHAPTER 22:

You Cannot Be an Eagle Christian without Singing

Almost all birds including eagles sing and it's a major part of most bird's lives. What's very interesting about birds singing is that they sing the loudest and most intensely just prior to flying at the crack of dawn. They start the day off with singing and soon after flying follows.

God has ordained Godly music to strengthen His children and refresh their weary spirits. Eagles and other birds teach us that if we start the morning off with singing in our hearts flying will be right around the corner. The Word of God is filled with verses expressing the importance of singing and if we desire a fresh renewing of spirit we must have a song on our lips at all times.

Godly music can drive away all doubt, fear, sorrow, and bondage and when we get born again singing will be a crucial part of our lives. Psalm 40:1-3 says, "I waited patiently for the Lord; and he inclined unto me, and heard my cry. He brought me up also out of a horrible pit, out of the miry clay, and set my feet upon a rock, and established my goings. And he hath put a new song in my mouth, even praise unto our God: many shall see it and fear, and shall trust in the Lord."

Just like with birds, God puts a song inside every Christian that gets saved. When God's children sing daily Joy comes inside, and others want to be around them. Singing has the ability to bring us into God's presence and without singing life is miserable. I've never seen a

Christian soar with God who does not saturate themselves with music from above.

Isaiah 35:10 says, "And the ransomed of the Lord shall return, and come to Zion with songs of everlasting joy upon their heads: they shall obtain joy and gladness, and sorrow and sighing shall flee away." Every great preacher, missionary, evangelist, author, saint, and laymen I've ever known have one thing in common, they have a song in their heart. The greatest preacher of his day, Mr. D.L Moody, once said he would trade all his accomplishments for one song Will Thompson wrote called "Softly and Tenderly." He said music has the ability to lift a heart out of the depths of sorrow more than anything else can.

If you are down and you feel you will never fly again, get a song in your heart and before too long everything will change. When folks refuse to sing in church they hinder others and themselves from soaring. Godly songs can open the prison doors in your life and you will find yourself shouting the victory for God's honor and glory. A Christian without a song spiritually is like a bird without wings physically.

God's music can drive away the demons that haunt people and the devil cannot handle Christians with praise on their lips. Never live in the past mistakes you've made, wake up every morning with a song on your heart and dreams of soaring and God will lead you every step of the way.

The birds have no worries and singing is the major reason why. Singing is a powerful force that can awaken the eagle inside any child of God. Psalm 149:1 says,

"Praise ye the Lord. Sing unto the Lord a new song, and His praise in the congregation of saints."

Don't let anyone steal your song of triumph, sing your way out of problems and allow the power of God to turn you into a new creature for His glory. When you live without singing you will never really live at all. God wants all Christians to sing for His glory and when we do He will take us to places we have never been before. If you want to enter into the presence of the King, open your mouth and begin to sing.

CHAPTER 23:

Eagle Christians Abide Under the Shadow of God's Wings

IRA David Sankey wrote 750 songs and gave up everything to help Mr. D.L Moody, the greatest preacher of his day. Sankey is known around the world and his impact is enormous and his songs have stood the test of time. Among his most famous songs is a song called "Under His Wings" and it shows the importance of God's children resting under the shadow of the Lord's wings.

The Bible says this in Psalm 91:4, "He shall cover thee with his feathers, and under his wings shalt thou trust: his truth shall be thy shield and buckler." Moses also said this in Exodus 19:4, "Ye have seen what I did unto the Egyptians, and how I bare you on eagle's wings, and brought you unto myself." Over and over throughout God's word, the Bible talks about eagle's wings and God's feathers and there are major reasons why.

If people really understand the power and safety that comes with being under God's wings they would swiftly try to hide in his comfort. Bald eagles have roughly 7,000 feathers that are granted them by the mercy of God. They are made to endure the rain and hold in warmth as well. Eagles have seven to eight feet wingspans and when a storm threatens their young, mom can stand on one side of the nest while dad stands on the other and they can stretch their wings over there young and it provides safety for their young eaglet.

Pound for pound the eagle wing is stronger than the wing of an airplane. Eagle feathers are designed tough yet soft and if you held 30 feathers in your hand they together would weigh less than a penny. When an eaglet is under his father's wing he has no worries, no fears, and is shielded from danger of any kind.

As God's children we need to allow God to take us under His wing because there is no greater place we could ever be. There are five things that you will feel when you're under God's wings and I want to list them now.

Number one, you will feel shelter from the storm. No matter what storm comes your way always remember His wings will block the rains from hitting you, and they will keep you safe from all harm. Under His wings you'll find warmth, love, security and comfort no matter how loud the winds of life hail and crash against you. The next time storms arise on your pathway don't panic, but rather get under His wings as fast as possible and peace will replace fear every time.

The second thing you will feel under God's wings is a nearness to the father like never before. Those who abide under the shadow of the almighty will always feel a nearness to God that others miss out on. Under the father's wings is fellowship, friendship, happiness and delight that gets stronger each day. If you want to grow in the grace of God get under His wings and you will experience a closeness to God like you have never known before.

The third thing you will feel under God's wings is the voice of the father himself. Many Christians will never hear God's voice in their life because instead of running to Jesus when trouble arises they run away from Him. When you're under His wings, God's words are not muffled, unclear, or hard to understand. When you're in the nest with the Father His voice can be clearly heard and there is nothing like hearing God's voice in our lives.

The fourth thing you will feel under His wings is unconditional love. There is no love that exists that is stronger than the love of our heavenly Father and the closer you stay to Him the more love you enjoy. Under His wings he comforts, spoils, pampers, and feeds us all the days of our life, and his mercies grow sweeter every day.

Lastly under His wings you can even feel the Father's heartbeat. Imagine being so close to the Father that you can hear and feel His heartbeat. The Bible declares that John the beloved often leaned on Jesus' breast and heard the heartbeat of God. Folks we all should desire to have that testimony in our life. Whenever John was in danger he was not ashamed or afraid to snuggle up to Jesus. Because John had this mindset Jesus allowed him to do and see things other never did.

John wrote St. John, 1st, 2nd, and 3rd John and the book of Revelation. Jesus also allowed John to take care of His mother because he trusted John and knew he would treat her with care and compassion. Out of all the symbols John could have had in the Bible He was given the symbol of the eagle. A man described that the symbol of an eagle is the highest form of inspiration one can have and John received that because he really loved God and had a seat right next to Him at the last supper.

My advice to anyone reading this chapter is to get under His wings every chance you get. When life is at its worst allow Jesus to take you into His bosom where there is rest from the devil's attacks. There is power, protection, and pleasure under the wings of Jesus Christ.

CHAPTER 24:
To Have Eagle Christianity You Must Be Committed

An eagle life is one of commitment and they are dedicated and serious about many things.

An eagle's life consists of flying, providing, protecting and giving their life for their family. When an eagle mates with another eagle it is for life and unless their partner dies they are committed to each other. Statistics say that around ninety percent of eagles mate for life.

Humans saved and unsaved need to learn from their example because the divorce rate in America is around sixty percent and commitment to one another is not as strong as it once was in this country. Eagles are also committed to their children and the mother and father spend most of their time investing in the future of their young. An eagle is always providing, and teaching their young ones how to grow, succeed, and eventually fly so that they can reach their maximum potential in life.

In America, family after family is failing to teach their children how to grow spiritually, and people are lovers of pleasures more than lovers of God. Mothers and fathers in these last days are not committed to the future of others but in many situations they seem to only care about themselves. People treat jobs, toys, games, sports, homes, cars, boats, and many other things better than they treat family, and God's house. People drop by the house of God whenever it is convenient and churches cannot flourish with this mindset. I know many stories of daddies spending more time at the local bar then they do with their family and a lack of commitment is killing this country.

An eagle's heart is totally committed to everyone except themselves and God will always honor anyone who thinks life this. We are living in the most selfish and self-centered days ever known in the history of mankind. An eagle like mindset is almost a thing of the past. We need commitment to God, family, and flying spiritually again if we want to make a difference in this dark world.

Flying for God is impossible without committed hearts and to be an eagle Christian you must not allow anything to stand between God, family and soaring to new heights. We must make up our minds every day to invest in the lives of others. Refuse to be lazy, and strive to do everything with total commitment and we will be a success all our days.

Eagle Christianity is available to any and all who decide not to quit when the storms of life come. If you commit thy works unto the Lord, thy thoughts shall be established, and your pathway will be ordered by the Lord.

Uncommitted people will destroy the home, the church, and the nation. An eagle's life teaches us all that victory, success, and production is a result of how committed we are. An eagle's passion carries them to heights others will never reach and many Christians will never be what God wants them to be because they won't surrender all to Him. The day we commit our lives to the Lord will be the day we become all we can be for God.

When an athlete puts in the work fully, he puts himself on the road to being a champion, and when a Christian does the same thing his best days are ahead of him. Give God your heart today and don't let anything rob you of a committed life. God give us an army of people who will let go of their own will, and commit everything to the Savior.

CHAPTER 25:

If you want to Have Eagle Christianity you must Be Rare for God

There is one thing you will never see an eagle do and that is apologize for being an eagle. An eagle will not fly at a lower lever just to make others feel better about themselves. There are only 70,000 total bald eagles that cover North America and if you're blessed to witness one in your area it will stick in your mind forever. Eagles are different, distinctive, and a rare jewel in every way. God has blessed eagles with amazing gifts that are meant to be displayed to all.

The Bible says, "We are fearfully and wonderfully made." God wants us to shine in the dark world for His honor and glory. When people want you to stop soaring and hang low with them, ignore them and soar as high as you possibly can. Misery loves company and those who are cold want to steal your thunder for God. If God is working in your life don't allow anyone to convince you to leave the air. Be rare, be special, and if others get upset just let them be upset.

A man said this years ago, "When you soar like an eagle, you attract hunters." When you're on the top, others will try to gun you down, but fly out of their sight and be rare for Jesus. Someone said this and I quote, "Eagles don't take flight lessons from chickens." Mr. Carl Sandburg once said, "There is an eagle in you that wants to soar."

Far too many Christians will never reach the peak of their potential because they don't believe they can. We need to get rid of negative influences out of our lives and once we do our future will be filled with   hope and promise.

Don't sell out your future of flight for doubt and fear. God loves you and he can empower you in ways that will leave others speechless. If you have rare gifts use them for God and if others leave you, well they weren't real friends anyhow. Desire to be rare and God will be the wind beneath your wings.

CHAPTER 26:

To Have Eagle Christianity You Must Have Backbone for the Lord

There is no one who has ever made a great impact for the Lord without think skin and a strong backbone for God. When you study how God designed man you discover that humans have seven cervical vertebrae and can rotate 70-90 degrees in either direction. Eagles on the other hand have fourteen cervical vertebrae, and can rotate 180 degrees giving them more flexibility to see in more directions. An average human weighs 191 pounds, while an average bald eagle weighs 10 pounds. Although a human weighs 19 times more, Eagles still have double the backbone and will always accomplish greater heights than mankind.

In the Christian life the majority of Christians won't stand against anything and they have the backbone of a noodle. Eagle Christianity will always have an advantage over Pharisee Christianity because it has double the backbone and can see in more directions with much clearer discernment. Christians are more concerned with being comfortable in sin and having buddies then pleasing God and doing His will.

When I think of backbone for God I think of the three Hebrew children who refused to take the easy route and went against everyone else who did. They looked at the people, the fire, and yes even the King himself and said we are not bowing to peer pressure and if we go down we will go down trusting God. Everyone thought they were ignorant rebels but God seen their boldness and walked with them through the flames and not one hair on their body was harmed.

Sometimes in life you will have to go against family, friends, authorities, and even leadership to stay in the will of God, and having backbone is a requirement to please God. David went against everyone when he took out Goliath and God said he was a hero not a stubborn Christian like everyone was labeling him as. People without backbone will always secretly fight against anyone who has it.

Daniel was falsely accused and cast into the den of lions because he took a stand for God. Martyrs by the untold, millions were brutally murdered because they were not afraid to expose evil and one day they will be honored in the heavenly courts of God.

We live in days where people don't want conflict or strife and they join the crowd of spineless jellyfish that accomplish nothing for God. We need an army of Christians to rise up with backbone that will stand up against anything or anyone who stands in the way of spiritual progress without fear of anything. Having backbone for God will never put you in the majority of popularity but a great man once said with God you are the majority. Dynamite comes in small packages but when eagles attack their goals an explosion of success will always be seen and heard.

Don't spend your life going with the crowd but spend your life standing for what's right and God will be a greater friend than anyone will ever be. Eagle Christianity may seem lonely to others but God sends peace in the midst of the storm and joy that abides forever. Be an Elijah who stood against the evil of his time and maybe you will be caught up in the chariot of fire one day.

Nothing great can ever be done without those who stand for what they believe in. obey God, stand strong and have a backbone like a telephone pole for God and the Lord will guide you towards eagle Christianity.

CHAPTER 27:

To Have Eagle Christianity We Must Have a Heart for God

As I look around America today I see fakeness everywhere. People forget that God is not interested in man's talent, smarts, education or knowledge, but he is interested in a man's heart. There are over 900 verses in the Bible that deal with the heart and those who pursue after him with pureness of heart will soar every time. People overthink, over analyze, and try to use your brain to advance with God but this will lead to many mistakes that will leave us powerless with God.

The Bible says David was a man after God's own heart and as a result he was worth 10,000 men and the greatest king Israel ever had. When you look how man and eagles were created you clearly see why one flies and one does not. When you follow after a heart for God it produces faith and spiritual wings. When you go after physical smarts it produces doubts and questions that leave us wondering what it's like to fly.

An average human's heart is 5 inches in length, 8 cm in width, 2.5 inches in thickness and 11 ounces overall. If you make a fist that is about the average size of the heart. However, a human brain is the size of two fists and weighs about three pounds. Humans spiritually will naturally use their brain more than the heart and it keeps them away from the skies spiritually speaking.

An eagle is totally different and operates in faith all his days. An eagle's brain is the size of a walnut and its heart is very large. The eagle doesn't rely on its own smarts but naturally uses the heart and flies higher than any bird flies. A human heart is about 0.4 percent of its total weight while an eagle's heart makes up about 4 percent of its total weight.

The Bible says without faith it's impossible to please him. So many people seem to have all the answers but in God's eyes they are lacking because their heart is black as coal. David said create in me a clean heart. Jeremiah 28:13 says, "And ye shall seek me, and find me, when you shall search for me with all your heart." Christians everywhere spend most their energy trying to impress others while all the time forgetting that God sees the heart.

A leech has 32 brains and they can suck blood for hours and hours until they are completely full. Spiritual leeches fill the land and they have one purpose in life and that is to suck the life out of everything they come in contact with. They will use all 32 brains and think of new ways to kill the church. A spiritual leech will never sing, worship, serve, smile, teach, give, support preach, witness or testify. Leeches will only think of new ways to drain others and destroy life as often as possible. There are millions and millions of leeches that cover the Earth and they have suckers on both ends. God doesn't need spiritually educated leeches. He needs more eagles with the heart as big as Texas.

There is only so far you can go with brain smarts but with a heart for God there is no limits of where God can take you. 1 Samuel 16:7 says. "Look not on his countenance, or on the height of his statue; because I have refused him: for the Lord seeth not as man seeth; for man looketh on the outward appearance, but the Lord looketh on the heart."

Humans commonly make the mistake of outthinking life, an eagle commonly forsakes his own wisdom and runs to the heart for direction. Those who are clean on the inside will always go higher than they ever thought they could.

CHAPTER 28:

Eagle Christians Choose to Soar Above Obstacles that Come Their Way

Job 14:1 says "Man is born of a woman a few days and full of trouble." All humans have afflictions they deal with but the great Christians refuse to throw in the towel and they allow God to turn their obstacles into an opportunity for him.

Psalm 34:19 says, "Many are the afflictions of the righteous: but the Lord delivered him out of them all." No matter what sin we face, trial we encounter, physical difficulty we endure, or spiritual mountain that stands in front of us we can soar over it all through the power of the Spirit.

Paul said "I will glory in my infirmities; that the power of Christ may rest upon me." Paul also said "Rejoice in the Lord always; and again I say rejoice." And when he wrote that he was writing in a dark, damp prison cell.

When you study an eagle's life you find a difficult pathway they must travel down. They have few friends, many enemies, and growing pains they must go through. They must deal with all kinds of weather, the death of some of their eaglets, and storms of all kinds. Naturally because they are kings of the air others hate them and try to fight against them.

When I think of eagles physical make up it's enough to make a stone weep. They have no teeth, no vocal cords, big beaks, a hole in their tongue, little stomachs, little brains, eyes that take up most of their head, extra weight they must carry, 106 degree temperature, wild hair days, no hands, hollow bones, 7,000 feathers, white head, brown body, and two feet with 4 toes on each foot. Eagles deal with obstacles that many couldn't handle but an eagle is great because it doesn't play the victim role but it plays the victor role and turns negatives into positives.

An eagle knows if he stays in the nest all day the opportunity to fly will pass him by. Instead of dwelling on his obstacles he will rise up and with a conquering spirit dominate the air with confidence and joy. We all have a choice as Christians, we can dwell on our problems and fall into depression, or we can dwell on the positives of life and experience triumph and victory each and every day.

Last year in America, billions upon billions of anti-depressants were sold to help people get over their problems. Millions every day will run the same problems through their mind and tears, like a river, will roll down their cheeks. Depression is basically a big pity party and if the devil can control your mind he can control everything else as well.

Eagles have no time for self-pity and instead of sitting around they tackle the world and stay active. For the majority of the eagle's life he is victorious and God wants us all to know what flying is all about. Problems will come, there is no avoiding that but when they do come remember Job 1:21, "That Lord gave, and he Lord hath taken away; blessed be the name of the Lord." Always think positive and always remember Jesus wants the best for you and he has a purpose for everything that happens good and bad. A man once said "Be kind to all because everyone is fighting a battle that we don't know about."

Eagle like all others have problems but because they handle it with class and integrity people only see a winner not a whiner. Eagles will spend their days in faith not fear and this quality propels them to fame. Some of the greatest champions for God were those who took their pain and turned it into praise and went on for the glory of God. Eagle Christianity is available to those who look at the tall mountain of fear, and consider it a stepping stone to greatness.

Nothing is too hard for the Lord and if you will allow him to handle your obstacles nothing will be able to stop you. If God be for us who can be against us. Be an eagle Christian and treat every day as a day to shine for Jesus Christ.

Anthony Ritthaler

CHAPTER 29:

To be an Eagle Christian you must Learn How to Fly Alone

What separates eagles from other birds is their contentment of flying alone. There is a famous quote that says this "Don't worry about being outnumbered, pigeons fly together, but eagles fly alone." An eagle will fly with other eagles but when it comes to flying with other birds they are not interested. God has filled an eagle's heart with uniqueness, bravery, and confidence and it does not compete or compare itself with other birds. Eagles, because of their size are at the top of the food chain and they don't mess with other birds.

An eagle does not need an army, a crowd, or a committee to survive but rather they depend on the wind to take them where they need to be. Eagles don't need the approval of others to thrive, they just fly alone and accomplish great feats without help from other birds. An eagle understands how to fly and it won't hang around anything that restricts them getting air borne. An eagle will not join the crowd that goes after dead things but it only goes after lively things. An eagle is happy to be an eagle and it is not worried about anything except flying as high as possible.

As Christians we should have the exact same attitude. God has called us out of darkness and has made us special through Jesus Christ. The Bible tells us to "come out from among them and be ye separate saith the Lord." We should all reach for new heights and we should obey God rather than man. When God saved us he placed in us the abilities to be eagle Christians and we don't have to settle for anything less. Christians love to have approval from man and they sell out power from on high for people that will bring them down.

To be an eagle Christian is lonely and people refuse to pay that price so they chose the easy route instead. The Bible says John was the greatest but he was alone with God before he even took flight in his ministry. David obtained eagle Christianity while taking care of sheep for his dad, away from the crowd. A great man once said "The greatest accomplish one can accomplish in life is to be there selves."

Churches are filled with clicks, committees, groups, and people that all band together to achieve their agenda. Most people want friends more than God's approval. God is looking on the inside not the outside of man and he knows who is real and who is not.

When you are an eagle Christian you will most likely not be popular but you will do things others can only dream of. John the Revelator was exiled to the isle of Patmos alone but on the island he wrote the book of Revelations. All throughout history the greatest Christians have been hated, despised, forsaken, abused, and killed but God took them to heights that staggered others.

Don't hang around negative people who never help, or assist you on your journey with God. If you have to fly alone so be it. Eagles are more concerned with soaring then they are having a crowd around them. Elisha asked for a double portion of power not people and if we want to be special for God we must desire the same thing. It's easy to take the easy route and hang with the vultures but if you chose to do so you will never reach higher ground.

Hang around others eagles whenever you can because they will motivate you to grow stronger for God. If people don't like it that's ok, do what the eagle does and fly without their approval. In Gods eyes its always far better to fly with the Lord alone then it is to feast on the dead with a crowd. Never apologize for being an eagle and live your life in total faith whether others do or not. Be yourself and don't worry about what others say. If you are around people that try to stop you from flying get away from them as soon as possible. Be all you can be for God and soar to the Heavens for His glory.

CHAPTER 30:

If you Desire to be an Eagle Christian you must be a Fisher of Men

It absolutely amazes me how eagles pursue after fish. Around 90% of what an eagle eats is fish and it attacks it with great passion. When an eagle hunts it looks effortless and smooth. People often send me videos of eagles swooping down and capturing fish and it looks graceful, majestic and easy.

Eagles use great vision, faith and the wind when they go after fish and if we want to be successful soul winners we must use the same methods. Jesus said in Matthew 4:19, "Follow me, and I will make you fishers of men." As Christians we are commanded to go after souls with passion like the eagles do. If we allow the Lord to teach us how to fish for men our spiritual nets will be busting at the seams.

Jesus said "without me ye can do nothing." And He would not even send his disciples out according to Luke 24:49 until they were endued with power from on high. God's children try to go fishing without God's strength, power, and assistance and come back frustrated and wore out. If you watch an eagle fish it's basically poetry in motion because they use Gods wind and energy not their own.

The greatest soul winners who have seen thousands saved all believed in going after men with a power that was not their own. Charles Finney seen the greatest harvest of fish get brought into the net in the shortest period of time due to the power of the Holy

Ghost. Over 600 thousand people were saved in fifteen months and people were making a difference for God. The fish are out there but they won't just jump in the boat. We have to go after them with purpose and hunger. Jesus said the harvest is plenteous but the laborers are few.

Eagles know that going after fish takes work, planning, drive, and determination but they also understand that their enemy is not going to drop them off for them. If the eagle stays in the nest he will miss out on fish so he will leave his comfort zone and search for them with extreme zeal and focus.

Fanny Crosby said it best when she wrote "Rescue the perishing care for the dying, snatch them in pity from sin and the grave." People all around us out slipping off into Hell and we must snatch them from the clutches of Satan. Jude said it like this" And of some have compassion, making a difference and others save with fear, pulling them out of the fire." If we can get a visual of how an eagle goes after a fish and apply it to our spiritual life we too can make a difference.

Eagle Christianity is all about casting out the spiritual net and rescuing as many as possible. Go after fish with all you got and you will be an eagle for the Lord. If we don't reach those around us no one will. Determine to fish for the souls of men every day and God will give you a great abundance for His glory.

CHAPTER 31:

In Order to Have Eagle Christianity You Must Hunger For Preaching

When a baby eagle is born they are born facing the sun. When an eaglet opens his eyes for the first time he immediately sees the father and the sun. From that time forward until they leave the nest they will be fed up to eight times a day and they got the choice to swallow the meat and live or choke on it and die. The mother and father will get food for the baby, break it up and feed it all in an effort to see the babe grow stronger and stronger until it flies.

When I read how they are fed up to eight times a day I thought of preaching immediately. The eaglet is not selective with the meat and the more they get the stronger they become. God has ordained preaching and if we want to fly one day we must consume as much of it as possible. I Peter 2:2 says, "As newborn babes, desire the sincere milk of the word, that they may grow thereby." We should feed on preaching every chance we get.

Don't wait until Sunday to feed on preaching. Get as many spirit filled preaching CDs as possible and feed on them over and over again, every day. The preaching of God's word is the spiritual fuel that drives us toward the sun. Preaching can fire us up, lift us up, move us up, and charge us up. The power of preaching can infuse us with strength, energy, boldness, and confidence to fly. Preaching can ignite a fire inside of us that causes us to reach for the stars.

When an eaglet knows its feeding time he gets excited, joyful, and jubilant and he enjoys every second of it. Christians all around this world need to take note of that and treat preaching the same way. Preaching should always be the number one attraction in Gods house and when we enter into the doors preaching should pump us like nothing else can. When your mind is on preaching every day you will be excited when Sunday rolls around. Most people look like death warmed over at church and that is because their minds are on everything except preaching. Billy Sunday said this, "The backslider likes the preaching that wouldn't hit the side of a house, while the real disciple is delighted when the truth brings him to his knees."

Eagles are fully mature in just a five year period and they are victors from there on out. If we fed on preaching eight times a day imagine how mature we could be for Jesus. Eagle Christians love preaching and they can't survive without it. Thank God for old time preaching, that gives us strength to soar.

CHAPTER 32:

Eagle Christianity is not possible Without Being a Great Giver

The power of giving can take any man, woman, boy or girl to heights with God that nothing else can. The Bible teaches that God loveth a cheerful giver, and when you study the Bible you will find many that advanced to great levels due to a giving heart.

In Mark chapter 14, we find a woman who gave her alabaster box to Jesus and the Lord took notice of it. This dear lady gave her year's wages to Jesus and this one act of giving took her from least in the room to greatest in the room in a matter of seconds. Luke 6:38 says, "Give, and it shall be given unto you; good measure, pressed down, and shaken together, and running over, shall men give unto your bosom. For with the same measure you that ye mete withal it shall be measured to you again." When you're a giver God can take you places that you never dreamed were possible.

Galatians 6:8 says" For he that soweth to the flesh shall of the flesh reap corruption: but he that soweth to the spirit shall of the spirit reap life everlasting." When a person is selfish they cannot be blessed of the Lord. But when a person is a giver spiritual blessings will burst forth like a fountain.

II Corinthians 9:6 says "But this I say, he which soweth sparingly shall reap also sparingly; and he which soweth bountifully shall reap also bountifully." I've seen people start out with nothing but end up with everything through the avenue of giving.

As you study the life of the apostle Paul you will find many people he listed that helped his ministry. Among the list of people you find a husband and wife that were dear to Paul's heart by the names of Aquila and Priscilla. God's hand was upon Aquila and Priscilla and the more they helped Paul the more God advanced them. They constantly gave to help Paul and even housed him for 18 months. Paul mentioned them a number of times in Scripture and because of giving they soared with God and was a part of one of the greatest ministries of all time. The name Aquila means eagle or eagle hearted. God took a regular man with a giving spirit and turned him into an eagle Christian.

If you're determined to give until it hurts, God can change you into something glorious for him. All throughout the ages of time God has blessed givers and the more you give the more God will open up Heaven for you. Malachi 3:10 says "Bring ye all the tithes into the storehouse, that there may be meat in mine house, and prove me now herewith, saith the Lord of hosts, if I will not open you the windows of heaven, and pour you out a blessing, that there shall not be room enough to receive it." When you give, God will always give more back.

Eagle Christianity involves giving to the cause of Christ. Without giving your power to fly will never come. When you decide to give, God can take the ordinary and make it extraordinary. Proverbs 3:9-10 says this, "Honor the Lord with thy substance, and with the firstfruits of all thine increase: so shall thy barns be filled with plenty, and thy presses shall burst out with new wine." Whenever you live a life of giving your barns will be full, your joy will be full and your flight schedule will be full. Be a giver and enjoy what it's like to soar with the Lord.

CHAPTER 33:

To Have Eagle Christianity You Must Encourage Others Not Discourage Others

One thing I love about eagles is the fact that they are meant to fly and they love when their eagle brothers fly too. Eagle are not jealous of other eagles and the higher they all fly the happier they all are. Eagles often fly alone but if they run into an eagle on their travels they will fly along each other enjoying one another's freedom. It is said that eagles can spot other eagles up to fifty miles away and if one is hurting they will do everything in their power to lift up the fallen and encourage their brother to soar like they used too. It is clinically proven that every single eagle at one point of their life will go through a dark valley of depression and no one knows why it just happens. When this happens an eagle will leave the air and become earth bound for the first time in their life.

You see God designed eagles to fly not walk and because they're not meant to walk their feet swell up and everything starts to break down from the inside out. They don't want to eat, fly, move, or even live and they end up in a valley and all their joy is gone. They give up on life as they lay on a rock and just stare at the sun. He lays there broken. Confused, depressed, miserable, and powerless. As his enemies laugh at him. He has no song, his shout is gone, and he doesn't even feel like an eagle. As he is considering death and he is at his lowest point in life all of a sudden he hears sounds coming from a distance that's familiar to him but he doesn't move. The sound that's getting closer is his fellow eagle brothers and they are coming to offer help to their hurting brother.

When the eagles finally arrive they are carrying meat in their talons and they all take turns dropping meat to the hurting eagle and one by one they do aerial tricks to encourage him to fly again. Next they start shouting words of encouragement and do everything in their power to offer help to their friend who is suffering. Eagle's greatest joy in life is to fly and see others fly with them. Eagle do not kick their brother when he is down and all the eagles offer encouragement and hope with every fiber of their being that the hurting eagle recovers for the glory of God. Sadly many eagles just give up but some are motivated to dust themselves off and take flight again.

The eagles hate to see their brother hurt and if the eagle recovers all rejoice and are thrilled. The encouraging shouts are from eagles who have already been through the valley and what they are telling the broken eagle is that if God can cause them to fly again, he can cause him to as well. Thank God for people that help others to reach their full potential and really want to be a blessing not a hindrance.

Churches all over this world are filled with people that discourage not encourage. Spiritual, judgmental Pharisees love to see others fall and enjoy every second of it. I cannot tell you how many people I talk to that tell me they quit on church because some person went out of their way to discourage them. Eagle Christians do their best to point people in the right direction with the spirit of love. Prodigal sons all over this world are not coming home because sadly they feel more love in the world than they do at church.

Pharisees love to glory in those who have fallen and throw wet blankets on those on fire for God. If you are guilty of this, eagle Christianity will never be part of your life. You can either be a Saul who tried to kill David and received an evil spirit or you can be tenderhearted, forgiving one another and experience blessings untold. It's completely up to you.

I'm going to encourage every eagle and non-eagle I see to be all they can be for the glory of God. The Bible teaches if we are spiritual we should help the hurting and lift up the fallen. Jesus told us to go the extra mile for others, and mend the broken hearts. Pastors are guilty of hurting people, members are guilty of hurting pastors. No one seems to repent and eagle Christianity wave's goodbye because of it.

God wants us to spend our lives building people up, not taring people down. Christians have no power to soar because secretly they are vultures not eagles and revival is a thousand miles away. God help us to drop meat, shout, and encourage those who have broken hearts. If we want to be eagles we must help others and do everything in our power to encourage them and God will honor our request to fly.

A man once said "We rise by lifting up others." And to that I say amen. Another said "The most beautiful people are those who bring out the beauty in others." We will never have God's touch until we have his heart. Folks be an encouragement and you will be a blessing to all.

CHAPTER 34:

If you Want Eagle Christianity Eliminate Discouragers from your Friend's List

The last thing an eagle needs in its life is drama so to avoid it they will fly alone away from the noise underneath them. The higher he flies the more freedom he feels and the more fulfilling his life will be.

Eagles don't stick their beaks in others business and kick their fellow eagles when they're down. An eagle is happy to be alone, but if they see another eagle struggling they will do their best to offer help. Eagle are not jealous of other birds, nor do they hang around them either. An eagle is a great encourager but many birds hate eagles because they can fly without a group, committee, or approval of others and this ticks them off. When jealously fills someone's heart they are capable of any evil imaginable.

A preacher once said "When Saul got jealous of David and God gave him an evil heart, from that day forward nothing David did could impress Saul." The preacher went on to say, "David could have walked on water and Saul wouldn't have cared one bit." The most dangerous person on Earth is not the drunk or the harlot, according to Gods word but it's the Pharisee that discourages others every chance they get.

If you study the life of Jesus his biggest problems came from the religious group who hated the fact that he exposed their secret life. The common man appreciated the Lord's power but nothing Jesus ever did impressed the Pharisees because their hearts were set on discouraging God's only Son. No miracle touched them, no sermon stirred them, His anointing meant nothing to them. Just think about it and let it dawn on you how evil this mindset and spirit is.

He walked on the water, they didn't care, He raised the dead, they hated him more, He made the blind to see, and they were mad as a hornet. Jesus made the deaf to hear and the Pharisees tried to stop him. The Lord fed the five thousand and the Pharisees tried to explain it away. Jesus preached the words of eternal life and the discouraging Pharisees accused Him of having a devil. Jesus Christ did everything a man could do to prove He was God but you never find a Pharisee getting saved outside of Nicodemus who had a change of heart. Pharisees were not there to help Jesus in anyway but they were there to try to stop Him from helping anyone else.

That my friend, is pure evil and when folks go out of their way to discourage others they are being controlled by the spirit of Satan. The more power you have with God the more discouragers will hate you. When you walk with power you will always have a target on your back as big as California.

When Elijah brought down fire from Heaven you would think people would be amazed by that but Jezebel had no fear and sought out to destroy the man of God and it brought discouragement to the point of Him wanting to die. When people are discouragers they don't respect a person on fire for God and they will band together with others with the same attitude and try to tear down, not build up. Encouragers build up the righteous, discouragers try to bring down the righteous and ignore every miracle in the process. Pharisees band together and cry out unity to the congregation but just because they are unified to perform their agenda, does not mean they love God. The Bible says as Stephen was preaching the crowd stoned him in one accord and at the same time gnawed on him like dogs and killed him.

To cover up secret sin in churches wicked members will try to silence the righteous and although they are in one accord they are evil in Gods sight. Joseph's brothers agreed to do away with their Godly sibling but just because they met together in unity does not mean they were right before God. Powerless Christianity rules the world today and to have power is rare to say the least. When you spend your life discouraging others true happiness can never be found.

Jesus called the Pharisees vipers, snakes, whited sepulchers, and dead man's bones. This world has seven billion people, surely we can find people who are an encouragement. Be like the eagle and refuse to hang around those who have no intention of helping you. Keep to yourself, fly alone, and be a blessing, not a hindrance and God will give you all the power you need.

The older I get, the easier it is for me to spot religious Pharisees. People who ignore power, miracles, and blessings, may look good on the outside but I promise you they are cold on the inside. Jesus rebuked discouragers over and over again because they had no problem grieving the Spirit of God, It's not the things we can see that kill revival, it's the things we cannot see that kills revival. People may carry a Bible, wear a suit or dress and have all the answers but if they are purposely hurting others they are blinded and dangerous to the cause of Christ. Discouragement is a great tool of Satan, don't allow him to use you as a wet blanket on someone else's fire.

Look to be a blessing and a spark for revival in other ministries and God's hand will rest upon you. If you want to fly with God you must get rid of the weight of discouragement that keeps you tied down. The more you encourage others will dictate how high you soar with God

CHAPTER 35:

To Experience Eagle Christianity you must shout the Victory

An old time man of God once said this and I quote, "Always remember Jesus is coming back with a shout and if it's good enough for Jesus it should be good enough for us. Psalm 47: 5 says "God has gone up with a shout." and I Thessalonians 4:16 tells us "The Lord shall descend from Heaven with a shout". In the Bible praise is found 246 times, rejoice 194 times, shout 72 times, dancing 19 times, joy 165 times, amen 133 times, and worship thousands of times.

There once was a time when people shouted the victory in Gods house and people ran the isles and could feel fresh power from above. Sadly those days are gone in the average church and if someone does have the boldness to shout, others talk behind their back and run them down the road. The devil hates when Gods children shout the victory and if you are in a church were one or two shout and all others don't you are in a mess and probably don't even know it.

I've felt incredible tension over the years for just enjoying God in church, but I know the importance of worship and I'm not serving man but trying to obey God. People have no problem shouting and getting excited over games, concerts, parties, or things they love but when they come to church they are half asleep and won't say glory to God even once. When we truly love God, worship will be a natural reaction in our lives. God is worthy to be praised and Jesus said "they that worship me must worship me in spirit and in truth."

When we come into God's presence we should come with thanksgiving, joy, power from on high, singing, love in our heart, and worship on our lips. If people would stop grieving the spirit and start enjoying the Lords presence we could see a great move of God again. We need an old fashion revival of Christians unplugging from worry and plugging into true worship. Statistics say in life most things we worry about will never come to pass but we allow the devil to rob us of our praise through worry, doubt, and fear. We need to get in the habit of worshiping God through the good times and the bad times because the truth is he is worthy at all times.

Although eagles don't have vocal cords they still make effort to create sound and they often scream and shout. There are three times when eagles shout and if we could make this pattern part of our walk with God, power could be ushered in for us. The first time Eagle's will scream or shout is when they want to scare off predators. Folks we have the victory and shouting will put fear into the enemy's heart and give us faith to go on flying for God.

The devil looks to pounce on those who are afraid to worship God and he will keep them weak and powerless. The devil don't want any part of a church that praises God and shouts the victory every time they can. The second time the eagle shouts is to warn other eagles of possible danger that is nearby. Eagles care for other eagles and when the spirit is right we will care for other people too.

When a man of God is preaching the truth and warning of danger around the corner we should shout him on and support the message. Real preachers will tell of danger close by and real eagles will shout him on. When danger is approaching others we need to shout the truth so they can make proper preparations to avoid being hurt. The last time eagles shout is while they are flying. Eagles will let off loud screams in flight to let others know they are enjoying freedom and are ruling that space of the air. Oh, how Christians need to shout to all those around them that they are not ashamed of Jesus and they are flying for His name.

When God is working in our lives we will shout the victory and the demons below will tremble. There is victory, freedom, and power in Christ and when you shout without fear of anything you will experience eagle Christianity. Psalm 150:6 says, "Let everything that hath breath praise the Lord." The great Billy Sunday said this, "take some of the groans out of your prayers, and shove in some shouts." He also said "If you have no joy there's a leak in your Christianity somewhere." God loves people that will endure the nasty looks from others and worship anyways. Eagle Christianity will never be reached without the attitude of praise and worship.

CHAPTER 36:

Eagle Christians Labor to Build a Mansion and are rewarded for doing so

An eagle's nest will always be a type of the mansions in Heaven because it's not built on the ground but rather in the air higher than all other nests. The largest nest ever recorded was 6.1 meters deep, 2.9 meters wide and weighed almost 6,000 pounds.

I'll never forget the first time God allowed me to see an eagles nest. Literally I stood there in awe beholding the massive structure and you could see it a mile away. After leaving that day I headed to a man's house and on his porch within arm's reach was a robin's nest that I could have held in my arms. As I thought on both nests one looked like it took endless hours and effort to construct and the other looked like it was whipped up in minutes. Eagle's nest have been called the mansion for birds and other kinds of nests will never match up to its strength and beauty.

In glory there will be robins who built little for God and eagles that labored with all their heart and built majestic mansions that all will behold. The judgement seat of Christ will separate the eagles from the robins and it may not matter to us now but five minutes in glory we will wish we built something that would have lasted.

Throughout an eagles life they will add more sticks and strength to their nest, to the point that it stands out to everyone around them. While others don't take it serious, precious time slips by, but an eagle takes advantage of its time and builds a mansion that lasts.

People will drive hours to see eagles nest but some won't walk across the street to see robin's nest and that's how Heaven will be. People who didn't take it serious and played around in their Christian life will be there but their efforts will turn into ashes. Others who gave it all for the Father will enjoy a mansion that all will long after.

John 14: 1-3 says "Let not your heart be troubled ye believe in God, believe also in me. In my father's house are many mansions; if it were not so, I would have told you. I go to prepare a place for you. And if I go and prepare a place for you, I will come again, and receive you unto myself; that where I am, there ye may be also." Some will have a glorious mansion that shines from the hills of glory, while others have a place down below. There is a huge difference between an eagle's nest and others.

God rewards those who spend their life building and he cannot do anything with anyone who doesn't work or labor for Him. In Matthew 6:19-20 Jesus said, "Lay not up for yourselves treasures upon earth, and where thieves break through and steal: but lay up for yourselves treasures in heaven, where neither moth nor rust doth corrupt it, and where thieves do not break through nor steal: for where your treasure is, there will your heart be also."

When mankind builds mansions down here in Gods sight it looks like a feeble robin's nest that will one day burn away. However, when eagle Christians labour and build for God they will have a palace awaiting them in glory and all the blessings that come with it. Always remember that in an eagles nest you will have fellowship with the Father, love, shelter under his wings, shelter from the storms, comfort on all sides, and the wind bidding you to fly.

One day if we labour for the Lord we will be perched high in the nest somewhere close to the Father while the enemy will be swimming in the lake of fire. The eagle is the strongest, the most successful, the hardest worker, and the most serious and as a result he is the king of the air, has the biggest mansion and is closest to the Father.

Set your affection on the things above and God will work alongside you to build something others could only dream of. Through God's spirit you will glide while others flap their wings. Thank God for the eagles nest for there is really nothing like it on Earth.

CHAPTER 37:

Eagle Christians Will Always Invest in the Next Generation of Eagles

Eagles are outstanding teachers and they are serious about training their young.

The Bible says "Train up a child in the way he should go: and when he is old, he will not depart from it." An eagles greatest desire is to see the youth fly one day and they will teach, train, love, impart wisdom, and encourage the next generation every chance they get. In the Bible we find the old time men of God investing in the youth, and teaching them to fly high for God.

Over and over again eagle Christians like Elijah taught Elisha the pathway to the air and Elisha received a double portion through Elijah's example. I could go through thousands of examples of great Christians training the youth to soar for God an if we want a true touch from Heaven we must do the same.

In these last days the older preachers have dropped the ball in this area and instead of encouraging a young eaglet Christian they go out of their way to discourage those with potential to do great things for God. Jealously, bitterness, and pride controls many hearts and as Saul tried to silence David, preachers all around this country secretly despise the youth with Gods touch upon their lives. Some of the most powerful preachers in this country have gone on record and said that consistently fellow preachers with a jealous spirit have been their biggest obstacle to handle in their ministry. Instead of training the youth to fly they will set them up to die.

143

There is no room in the ministry for head games, manipulation, lies, deceit, and trickery. Those who discourage the youth will pay for it.

Spirit filled eagles will inspire others to greater heights and they will not be the wet blanket on anyone's fire for God. When I think of the great Burlington revival that has brought revival to thousands around America I see hope for a broken country. Many have said the power is from another world and God has placed a hunger in the saved to carry the gospel to the lost. God has raised up a young couple that is doing their best to reach others and the key to that revival spreading is support from older Christians in that area. In one night of the revival over 400 preachers met under that tent and supported the revival.

Some preachers drove over nine hundred miles to be in the meeting and thousands have been transformed as a result. God has sent revival because not only the people are supporting the meeting but eagle preachers are as well. Folks if we ever want to see revival sweep across America again this pattern must continue the older has to support the younger, it's so important. Many older preachers will doubt this meeting, fight this meeting, and hate this meeting and because of that spirit God will cause their ministry to dry up and die.

Eagle Christians will always seek to invest in the youth and they will not hold them under their thumb. Leadership all around this country control others through fear tactics, mind games, and bully pulpits and they may look like eagles to others but in God's eyes they are nothing but turkey vultures. The older must take the younger under their wing and teach them how to fly.

Aaron had Moses, Johnathan had David, Timothy had Paul, and the disciples had Jesus.

Eagle Christianity is supportive, encouraging, kind, pure, and real and God's touch will always be upon them. If you are a pastor, leader, or member and you purposely hurt the youth that loves God you will never know anything about power from on high and judgement will always be nearby. If you're natural tendency is to stop someone on fire for God this verse is the sad testimony of your life: Psalm 66:18 says, "If I regard iniquity in my heart the Lord will not hear me. " Be an eagle and lift others up and you will be blessed all the days of your life.

CONCLUSION

As we conclude this book I want to thank you for your support, prayers, and efforts that make this all possible. Every one of you are precious to me and I am humbled that you took the time to read *Eagle Christianity.*

Please continue to pray for me on this writing ministry because the longer it continues the more Satan hates it. My prayer is that this book opened up things that you have never known before and I also pray it gave you a hunger to be an eagle for God. Eagle Christianity is meant for all but so very few care enough to experience it for themselves.

Without God's power we will only get the leftovers that remain but we will never enjoy the manna from above. Without God's anointing we will never reach full potential and we will never fully enjoy the life God has planned for us. God help us to apply the qualities that eagles possess and may we all fly for the glory of almighty God.

Life is too short and God is too good to waste our life away. Eagle Christianity will carry us to the very throne of God if we will allow it too. A great man once said "Leaders are like eagles, they don't flock together, you will find them one at a time." If you must serve alone, so be it. It's much better to fly with the Lord then it will ever be hanging with the dead.

Someone once said "You will never see an eagle of distinction flying low with pigeons of mediocrity." Whether anyone joins you or not, fly anyways. God will be your friend whether others are or not and if you soar with Him nothing else will matter in the end.

A man once said "many times it happens we live our life in chains and we never knew we have the key." Folks I got good news! God took the keys from Satan and if we will allow Him to unlock us from our prison of doubt and fear we can have eagle Christianity.

Here is a quote I love, "If you associate with eagles, you will learn how to soar to great heights. But if you run with dogs, you will learn how to bark." We need less barking and more soaring, less talking and more flying. Strive for higher ground with God and the Lord will teach you how to fly. May God bless you all in a great way!

God bless you,

Bro Tony

Anthony Ritthaler

CPSIA information can be obtained
at www.ICGtesting.com
Printed in the USA
FFHW021321111118
49302629-53538FF